"Sarah Birnel's *Something Better Brewing* isn't just a story about surviving a meth-infused adolescence. No, it's more like the author puts it into overdrive, totally kicks ass and ends up taking on the world and making it her own— one bikini-clad barista at a time. If empowered women success stories are your thing, then you're in luck, because it doesn't get any better than this."

— Patrick O'Neil, author of *Gun, Needle, Spoon*

"I was gripped from the beginning of this book. For anyone who feels like they can't get clean because the odds are against them, read this book. It will give you hope you can change."

— Nancy Carr, bestselling author of *Last Call*

"Sarah's honest journey breaks you open to see not only the underlining dynamic of addiction but also the view of fighting for life, recovery and the ability to live a life you are worthy of living. It breaks you open and then gives you cold chills, inspiring you to take one step out of your trenches at a time and to know, without a doubt, you can not only survive but also thrive."

— JAYDEE GRAHAM, MSSW, CSW AND BESTSELLING AUTHOR OF *THE SOUL GRIND*

"A vital, timely and unapologetic memoir of how one woman turned her tragedy into triumph. Sarah's transformation from prisoner to professional provides real hope for anyone questioning their ability to change the trajectory of their life."

— MICHELLE SMITH, AUTHOR AND FOUNDER OF RECOVERY IS THE NEW BLACK

"A wonderful story of resilience and hope as well as one of the best drug addiction memoirs and success stories of women in recovery out there."

— SAMANTHA PERKINS, AUTHOR OF *ALIVE AF: ONE ANXIOUS MOM'S JOURNEY TO BECOMING ALCOHOL FREE*

To Carter
Dandridge

something better brewing

What I Learned from Prison, Parenthood and Pouring Coffee

SARAH BIRNEL

launch pad
PUBLISHING

Copyright © 2021 by Sarah Birnel

All rights reserved.

No part of this book may be reproduced in any form or by any electronic or mechanical means, including information storage and retrieval systems, without written permission from the author, except for the use of brief quotations in a book review.

ISBN: 978-1-951407-64-3 paperback

ISBN: 978-1-951407-63-6 ebook

DISCLAIMER

This work is non-fiction and, as such, reflects the author's memory of the experiences. Many of the names and identifying characteristics of the individuals featured in this book have been changed to protect their privacy and certain individuals are composites. Dialogue and events have been recreated; in some cases, conversations were edited to convey their substance rather than written exactly as they occurred.

*For my parents
Rick & Cook*

CONTENTS

Introduction   xiii

1. Growing Up in Abuse   1
   Isn't an Excuse for Bad Behavior
2. The Road to Hell   13
   Is Paved with Bad Decisions
3. Hitting Rock Bottom   31
   Where at Least the Foundation is Solid
4. Believing in Yourself   46
   Takes a Whole Lot of Time, Work and Energy
5. Building a Business   62
   Is Hard as Fuck!
6. Going Back to Basics   77
   Can Solve Everything
7. Finding the Right Person   90
   Can Change Everything
8. Confronting Hard Times   98
   If You Lived Through That, You Can Live Through This
9. Other Women Aren't The Enemy   107
   No, Not Even the Hot Ones
10. Looking Forward   117
    Focusing on My Family and Myself

Acknowledgments   133
About the Author   137

INTRODUCTION

My left hand grips the bar of the stretcher as the nurse wheels me into the operating room. I try to hold on with my right hand but the handcuffs are too tight. I am wheeled behind a thin curtain where another inmate lies in a bed.

The nurse isn't unkind but treats with me the same bored frustration that most prison staff offer to the inmates—like a parent whose children are up past their bedtime. The nurse explains to me what's going to happen next but I barely hear the words—sedation, dilation, abortion. I nod because the choice has already been made. I am facing six years in prison. I have lost custody of the two sons I already have. And though I am now 20 weeks pregnant and none of this feels right, I also know I can't bring another child into the disaster that is my life.

I turn my head away as tears battle with my eyelids. I shut my eyes tightly. I can't cry. I can't feel this. I just have to wait for the sedation and then it will be better.

Since the age of 12, I have been waiting for the sedation, the easy drug to take me away, to make the world seem right even though it is so fucking far from it. And it's no different now as I wait for the nurse to slip the needle into my IV. Unlike with my boys, I think, I won't know when they remove this baby from my womb. I correct myself: *Fetus, not baby.*

I believe we all have the right to choose but somehow this doesn't feel like a choice.

My grandmother is already overwhelmed raising my sons. She has told me that there's no way she can take a third. And what is the other option? Foster care? I don't want that life for this baby—this fetus. And I don't want to burden my grandmother even further. This is the better way.

Maybe I belong in prison, safe and removed from the world, where I can't hurt anyone and where they can't hurt me.

The nurse leaves the room without administering the drug and I have an unexpected few minutes alone.

Do I call it off? Do I go through with it?

Do I keep living like this?

And that's when it happened. I can't say it was a white light moment because there was no light, no voice of God—just the slightest glimmer of something

I hadn't felt in a long time: change. Maybe this wasn't the life I was supposed to be living. Maybe my life was meant to be the kind of life that, for so long, I couldn't have even imagined.

I could stay sober. I could be a good mom. I could be out of prison. I could live a different life. A better one.

As the nurse came back in with the needle and slid it into my IV, I wondered if those thoughts would disappear after this day was over—but when I emerged from the procedure, groggy and no longer pregnant, filled with sadness and a questioning regret, I still hadn't forgotten that other feeling.

It felt like I had spent decades walking through a barren desert of my own drug use, my own trauma, my own bad decisions. And the worst part was, I didn't think it would ever be any different. I expected that I would live and die in that desert.

And then suddenly, almost miraculously, I was thirsty for change.

What happened next is the story I'm about to tell. But first, I'll back up. I'll show the twists and turns that ultimately led me into that desert. I'll tell you about the night my mother died. I'll tell you about what happens when you're a teenage drug user running the streets, looking for someone to save you.

I'll share about abandoning my own children and disappointing everyone I ever loved—and feeling like I was doomed to repeat the mistakes so many of my family members had already made.

But I'll also tell you what happens when all that changes. Because what I have realized in my journey after that cold and rainy morning, waiting for the nurse to sedate me from my own worst decisions, is that love is always there, like a waiting oasis, if you're willing to come in from the desert. If you're thirsty enough for it.

Over the next 15 years, I started living my life in reverse. I built a business that also became a community. I fell in love with a man who became my partner and friend and yes, sometimes also my savior. I created a family and raised three children (the third of whom was just born last year). I began to dig deep into what makes us unhealthy—emotionally, psychologically, physically.

As I continued to take more accountability for my life, I began to realize that our outcomes are always influenced by our decisions. Are we making the right choices for ourselves or are we making the wrong ones? Are we choosing to be healthy, committed and kind? Or are we trying to get what we can get and leave the rest behind?

Whether I was building my business or my family, I saw that the longer I stayed healthy, the more committed I became to my new life. I no longer spoke the same language as my old friends. I got a new address. A home. There, I could finally become the person I was always meant to be—not the little girl who grew up too fast, watching her family fall apart, not the pregnant 16-year-old who was thrown down a stairwell or the 21-year-old who aborted a 20-week old fetus. Not the girl in the orange jumpsuit, locked up and unsure if she'd ever get off the dangerous merry-go-round that her life had become.

I became an entrepreneur. A mother. A community leader. I became devoted to the health and wellness of my family and myself. I became the person that my mother, in her lucid moments, dreamt I would become.

It all started when I became thirsty for change.

And it can happen for you too.

We all have our own prisons. We have all wandered into the darkness, believing there was no way out. We have all been hurt, hurt ourselves, hurt the people we love. If you have actually been in prison, your sentence may end the day you are released—but what happens then?

The beauty of rock bottom is that it's a strong foundation for growth. We get to discover new lives. We can use the skills we learned inside to build companies, to make money, to take care of our families, to heal.

We can get better. We can change. We can start with small shifts and better decisions.

I didn't walk out and get it all right. I used again. I

hung out with the wrong crowd. I almost lost my business and my husband and I never got custody back of those two boys. There's still plenty I'd like to change about myself. But over time, I did begin to heal. And so can you.

I hope this book can be a mirror, reflecting back to you who you are and where you've been. Because regardless of whether your prison was a concrete building with too many loudspeakers and not enough towels or just the looming walls of your own mind, we all get to take ownership of our journey. We get to take back our shame and our blame and our dirty street games.

And we get to become the women (and men) that our mothers, even those who weren't always lucid, wanted us to be.

The more we heal, the better we are able to provide our children with the lives we had always hoped for for ourselves.

The bottom of the ocean might be rock bottom but the sea is made of love.

I look forward to swimming with you. It's going to be a fun adventure, even when it's hard. Like life. Like love. Like change.

1

GROWING UP IN ABUSE
ISN'T AN EXCUSE FOR BAD BEHAVIOR

"Mom! Mom!!!! Mommmmmmm!"

I heard my sister screaming before I knew what was happening or what was about to happen. I could hear furniture crashing on the floor above me, but this wasn't anything new. My mother had been using for days and my dad had come home to find the usual horror story—all of us kids living in filth and dirty dishes and drug paraphernalia. He had gotten tired of fighting for us; instead he would just fight directly with my mom, still believing that she could hear him—that somewhere in the depths of her addiction and mental illness, his voice might pierce, and she would realize what she had become and what she was doing to us.

Instead, she usually responded like most addicts—angry and defensive. And in my mother's case, violent.

She never hit us kids. Even when she was high out

of her mind, her love for us somehow always calmed that impulse. But when it came to my dad, she was entirely different. We had gotten to the point where we would hide anything that looked even remotely like a weapon, afraid of what she might do to him when he came to visit, even when he was bringing her things she needed, like food or clothes or money.

My father refused to give up.

Maybe he just couldn't give up the woman he married, the mother we also remembered, who was filled with joy and laughter, who cooked and danced and kept us all entertained. Even when the drugs took over, she was still funny, still a light even in all that darkness.

My parents had met in California. They both came from hard places. My mom was from Canada, of Native descent. She had long, dark thick hair. One eye was green, the other brown. She was thick and sturdy like a big brown tree. She came from a family of alcoholism and abuse, landing in Los Angeles after fleeing an abusive relationship in Canada, my oldest sister in tow. When she met my dad, it was as close as a woman like her could come to a fairytale.

Unlike my mom, my dad was tall and wiry. I think when he met her, he felt grounded by her. My dad's family had similar struggles. He was raised in Spokane, Washington but headed to LA as soon as he could, to party and have fun and put his childhood behind him.

My mother was the life of that LA party. They quickly fell in love and got pregnant, returning to Spokane where my dad started a carpeting company and my mom became a housewife. They bought a house in a neighborhood much nicer than anything either of them grew up in and for those first few years, it looked like they were both getting to do things differently.

Upon landing in Spokane, my mom decided she wanted to quit drinking.

"We both should," she told my dad. "We have a real chance here. We can build a home, raise a family. But we need to do it together."

My dad agreed, focusing on building his business. My mom got pregnant again. Everything was going great for a while. But then some evenings my dad would come home and there would be an empty wine bottle on the kitchen table. And by the time she had my sister Courtney, her fourth child, she had started taking pills. And the funny thing about addiction: as dramatic as it sounds, it's easy to overlook because it starts off so slowly. It's not like she was messed up every night—not at first. And in a way, with my mom drinking, my dad got to do what he wanted to do. He would date other women. He even brought some home. My mom would treat them like family as she floated around, high on beer and pills.

By the time she had my youngest sister, other drugs had begun to show up—cocaine and later, meth. My dad couldn't ignore it anymore.

"Cook, you've got to slow down," he would say. She would just wave him off. She was the boss and they both knew it. And my dad wasn't the only one stepping out. By the time I was eight, my mom had a serious boyfriend and no one could pretend we were a normal family anymore.

Sometimes I think of how it must have looked for our neighbors. My dad would get in the family car each morning and drive to the carpet store, returning home in time for dinner. My mom would shuttle us between school and soccer practice and music lessons. From the outside, we appeared to be the perfect upper-middle class family. But on the inside, things were very different. My sisters and I often wondered if our mom was going to die. A steady stream of strangers visited our house—dealers, boyfriends, girlfriends, drug buddies—and all of them came from rougher neighborhoods than the one we lived in.

Still, if you had asked any of us if our parents loved us, we would have immediately said, "Yes, more than anything." In spite of our chaotic environment, our home was also fun and loving and filled with laughter.

When my sister Jezi turned 14, she started using

with my mom. Mom didn't like to party alone, so if there wasn't a strange friend or boyfriend around, that left us. That first year, my mom introduced Jezi to alcohol and weed and then later, meth. I wasn't sure what was going on, but suddenly I noticed that my older sister had started acting a lot like my mother. It was like she had joined her secret club. When I turned 10, I followed her there.

My mom taught me how to drink, and it wasn't a big deal when I started smoking cigarettes and weed.

When my dad wasn't home, she did most of her using with her new boyfriend, Jordy. At that point, using was normal for us, but having some guy around who wasn't our dad (and clearly didn't appreciate having four little girls interrupting his time with his lady) was a sign to us that something wasn't right.

When you're 10 years old, you may not realize that you shouldn't be drinking booze with your mom, but you do realize she shouldn't be sleeping with another man in the bedroom she shares with your dad.

And then my mom got pregnant.

She was in love with Jordy and she wanted the baby to be his (though she couldn't actually be sure, because Jordy wasn't the only guy she was seeing) and she wanted my dad out. Though my dad earned all the money, once again, my mom was the boss.

The day we watched his car pull out of the driveway was the day we all knew our lives would never be the same. I mean, none of us would have predicted the eventual outcome, but we knew that any hope of us being normal, however delusional, was now over.

My mom knew it too. As much of a mess as she had become, my dad had a stabilizing effect on her and the household. Now that he was gone, it was just my mom, Jordy, the drugs and no rules.

My dad would sometimes come home to try to create order—cleaning the kitchen, checking in with us girls.

He knew that she was using a lot of meth, and after the new baby was born, it only got worse. She was in meth psychoses a lot of time, convinced that people were following her. She would drive around at night with the newborn Shelby in the car. My dad started going directly to the meth dealers, begging them not to sell drugs to her. Somehow my mom always found out, which only intensified their arguments when he came by the house.

He wanted to take us but, he knew that would have been an uphill battle, and he didn't want to put any of us through that, especially knowing that some of the kids weren't biologically his, even though he considered himself a father to all of us. By then my sister Jezi was almost 16, so even though my mom was checked out, there was someone close to a normal adult in the house. Even if given the chance, I don't think any of us would have wanted to leave anyway. We wanted to take care of Shelby and I didn't want to be away from my mom.

Jezi already had her own life—pregnant, she had moved in with her boyfriend. There were other people around: Jezi's best friend, who was like a sister to me, and my own foster sister, with whom I shared a room. But the most important person to me was my mom. Sure, I had friends at school, including my best friend who I had known since I was five, but my mom was my everything. That's the thing about living with an addict—you live in such fear of what they're going to do to themselves that you can't imagine leaving them, no matter how unhealthy they get. I knew something was wrong with her, but I also didn't know any other kind of life.

If my mom was a symphony, she was hitting the crescendo. It seemed like having Shelby had put her over the edge. At one point she had been an amazing mother—nursing us and cooking for us, braiding our hair and sewing clothes for us. But now for the first time in almost five years, she had a newborn to take care of and she could barely get out of bed—not to mention all the normal hormonal reactions to new motherhood.

My mom just couldn't take it.

The partying increased and so did the paranoia.

She'd always had a violent side. I can still hear my

dad pleading with her, "Cook, calm down. Calm down."

Once, our family dog scratched a neighbor's truck and that neighbor kicked our dog. Two seconds later, my mom was storming across the front yard and sucker punched the guy, who immediately retreated. But she was also the one to rescue people, often bringing in kids from abusive homes (as crazy as ours was, it was also safe).

Sure, I might have been drinking my mom's alcohol, but no one snuck into our beds at night and no one hit us. Every time my father came over, it almost felt like old times. When my mom and Jordy broke up, we all began to hope those old times would return.

But I also knew that my mom saw my dad as her biggest threat. As long as he was gone, she could use drugs without anyone stopping her.

My dad bought a river house and had planned on moving in. My mom showed up with Erin and Shelby, somehow having caught wind of the fact that he was going to live there. She totally lost it, and was swinging a knife around—he quickly decided the river house plan wasn't going to happen. .

But no matter how many times my mom yelled at my dad to leave or to stay away, he couldn't. Partially, this was because he loved us and was worried. As much as he was afraid to take us away, he was just as terrified to leave us there.

I also know my dad stuck around because he loved my mom. Up until her dying breath, she was the great love of his life. He always hoped that something might change and there were enough glimmers of light to keep his hope alive. She would quit drinking for a few weeks. She would quit the meth and begin to calm down. She would let him come over and thank him for the groceries. All of us—my dad, my sisters and me—thought each time might be the time it stuck, that we might really be a family again. That my mom's using and her other boyfriends and the chaos that sometimes overtook our home would turn out to be a bad dream.

One evening, my dad came over. It was the night of my sister's birthday. He was playing with the baby and watching TV—he and the younger girls were going to sleep in the living room. Even Jezi was there spending the night.

My mom finally got home at 3 in the morning, and he knew something was amiss. I don't remember him going through my mom's purse, but when she got home, I heard him talking to her in the kitchen.

"Where did you get this?" My dad must have held out the baggie of meth.

"It's none of your fucking business," my mom responded, grabbing her drugs back.

"Jesus, Cookie. How much more of this can we take? The girls? The baby?"

My mom couldn't take that line of questioning. I am sure it dug into the deepest part of her shame and like a lot of people, she responded to her own guilt with anger. She started accusing my dad of stalking her.

I don't know at what point my mom pulled out the butcher knife. All I could hear was the sound of furniture being pushed across the floor and my dad repeating like a mantra, "Cook, calm down. Cook, Cook, Cook."

Suddenly the dogs were barking and I heard my sister Jezi, screaming, "Daaaaadddd! Daaaaaddddd!!!! Daaad."

I could still hear my dad saying "Cook, Cook, Cook," but this time it was a question.

My sister Erin and I ran in to see what was happening. The lights were out, but I knew my mom was laying in the middle of the room. I ran to her, putting my head to her chest. It was dark but I could feel her. I could feel where the knife had stabbed her. I heard her gasping for breath. My dad was in a corner, in shock.

"She's breathing!" I yelled. Or at least, I think I did. I remember the rest of the night like shards of glass, my memory broken by what we did and didn't do. I know I got some towels. I tried to call the police but I was so worked up that I tore the phone right out of the wall. My younger sister Courtney was still hiding behind the couch when Jezi's boyfriend turned on the lights. My mom was lying there in a heap.

Later my dad would explain that when she attacked him, he had fallen on top of her, with the knife twisting backward and into her side.

I don't remember leaving the room but I was standing outside when the cops came, covered in her blood. I don't remember being with her when she took her last breath. I'm not sure that anyone was.

The police arrested my dad immediately. I remember watching him getting into the back of the squad car and knowing it was a mistake. I knew that my dad would have never deliberately hurt my mom. Jezi explained that when they were wrestling over the knife, the dogs were barking and circling their legs. That's when my dad tripped, landing on top of my mom and the knife. A priest came over and told us that our mom was dead, but we already knew that. In some ways, I was heartbroken but in other ways, I knew it had only been a matter of time.

That's the thing about addiction. You live in so much fear that the addict is going to die that at some point, you just come to expect it, to anticipate it. You know where all of this is going to lead eventually. But the one thing we didn't expect was to lose our father too. Even though it had been almost a year since he had moved out, he had remained a constant fixture in our lives.

He ended up posting bail but nothing was for certain—a trial was still looming ahead. We were released back into his care and moved into his house. Our aunt and grandmother often came over to help out too. I felt so angry at my mom, a feeling that had started before she died. Cookie was the addict. Cookie was the violent one. Cookie was the problem. But Cookie was also our mother. And for the first time, I was without my mother, and so were my little sisters. I was so tough, but the pain of them growing up without a mom was intense. One day, I left the house and didn't look back.

I wanted to remove myself from this reality so no one could find me. So that I could feel nothing. I wanted to join my mom. I became hell-bent on self-destruction.

Some kids leave home and start smoking pot, but I had been smoking pot for two years. I already drank. From time to time, I took acid. My only rebellion was meth, so I went off into the streets with a death wish, determined to become a junkie.

Just the year before, my sixth grade teacher had told my parents that I was upfront. When I wanted something, I would go get it. He was right, and it's still true today. But at 12, all I wanted to do was die.

In the space of three months, my father not only lost his wife but he was about to lose his daughter too.

2

THE ROAD TO HELL
IS PAVED WITH BAD DECISIONS

Everybody has a talent and I quickly found out mine was being a druggie. It wasn't a surprise since I had already been in training for years, but now that no one was paying attention, I wanted to try everything. And I had a perfect partner in crime.

Some people find drug buddies, lower companions that will shoot you up and then steal your dope. But I was lucky. I had my best friend Taryn. Taryn and I had known each other since fifth grade and like any kids with secrets to protect at home, we connected. We didn't have to talk about the trauma to both know it was there. But whereas no one in my house had gotten beaten or sexually abused, Taryn's home was a far more fucked up place to live. Her uncle had been molesting her and her sister for years. I convinced her that this wasn't a secret she should keep. She eventually told her parents about what had happened and even called the police but her family sided with her uncle, even after he was convicted and served time. Even before my mom died, Taryn spent a lot of time at our house. In a way, she also lost a parent when my mom died. As addicted as my mom was, there was always a part of her you could trust. Her home was open to anyone in need and Taryn had been deeply grateful for the safe harbor.

Now, for both of us, it was gone.

So together, we ran off. We used until we couldn't use anymore. We started shooting meth. One night, we found ourselves in the house of a child molester but it was cold outside and we didn't have anywhere else to go. We stayed in the same bed and kept watch over each other.

Some days were still fun. There was one snowy day in January where we were tripping on mushrooms and making snow angels. For a few hours, I could forget what had happened just the August before. In that world, my mom was still alive. My parents were still together. Maybe later that day, I would go home and my mom would be making dinner and singing in the kitchen while my dad played with us kids....

But that world was over. I lived in a new world now. The runaway world.

Sometimes I would go home and my dad would always let me back in, pleading in the same voice that he did with my mom, "Sarah, please, you can go to treatment." He had spent so much time chasing my mom around, begging her to get help, and it hadn't worked. Now here I was, his daughter, facing the same problems she had. He loved us so much, but he just didn't know what else to do. And maybe there's nothing he could have done.

I would nod and tell him I was tired, usually falling asleep while he sat on the edge of my bed, telling me how scared he was for me. I knew he didn't want to see me wrestle with the same demons that had overtaken my mom, but I also knew it was too late to stop that from happening. It had already begun.

One night, I ended up in the apartment of a weird man who made me sleep in his bed. I was almost 14 and still a virgin. Though Taryn and I had been on the streets for over a year, I hadn't had sex with anyone. I told the man I wanted to go home and he pulled out a gun. I knew what was next.

But instead, he just wrapped his body around mine, the gun in his hands, his dick hard against my leg. He fell asleep. In the early morning, I pretended to go to the bathroom and snuck out the front door while he slept. I later found out he was a pimp and was trying to groom me to become one of his girls. I never went back to his place, and unlike a lot of girls on the streets, I never got into sex work.

The following year, I had sex with a guy who I

thought I loved but really, my main purpose in life was to use. Taryn ended up meeting a drug dealer. We were 14 and he was probably in his early 20s but no one cared. Most people didn't realize how young we were anyway. Now when I see a 14-year old girl, I can't believe we survived in that world.

For me, my greatest weapon was my ability to use. I would use so hard, guys wouldn't even want to stick around.

"You're gonna die doing that and I'm not going to be here when you do," they would warn before hightailing it out of whatever bedroom or basement or alley we happened to be in.

Sometimes I would break into my dad's house to steal money. Once, I stole the family video camera, failing to empty the videos out of the bag—videos of my mom and dad and sisters, back when we were all together, back when it was fun. Another time, I found my grandma's purse and stole a check from it.

My sisters would sometimes track me down on the street, drag me back home and throw me in the shower like a flea-ridden dog. They would get angry at me, yelling, "Don't you think Dad's been through enough? How much more do you want to do to him?" I didn't have an answer.

On one of these occasions, I had been home for a couple of days and ended up going with my sister to one of her friends' houses. At some point, I got ahold of a speed ball. I remember locking myself in the bathroom because I thought people were after me. I was picking at my face in the mirror while my sister knocked at the door, trying to get me to come out.

I remember going outside and seeing an abandoned car in a field. If I looked at it from one perspective, I saw all my friends in the car but then the next moment, they would all be gone. Finally, someone called my dad and he came and took me to the hospital.

I was given a heavy dose of Valium at the hospital to bring me down but the trip didn't end. They diagnosed me with chemically induced schizophrenia. I was seeing people who weren't there. I thought for a part of the trip that my dad was one of my drug buddies, that this whole thing had actually been a set-up. I didn't know how to make it stop, but I also wasn't sure what was real and what wasn't. The doctors weren't sure how long it would last or if I would ever get better. Some of the things that happened during that trip are things I'll never forget, including the fact that at one point, I shaved off half of an eyebrow. And eyebrows take a long fucking time to grow back! So I guess I should be grateful it was only half of one? They held me in a padded room for a few days until the visions started to dissipate. They agreed to release me under the condition that I go to treatment.

At that point, I had been out of school for two

years. I hadn't seen a doctor. It was rare I would take a shower or stop using long enough to even know where I would be sleeping the next night. I floated around town from house to house, couch to couch.

I will never forget the look on my dad's face when he drove me to treatment. He was quiet in the car; maybe after all the years of begging my mother, he knew his words wouldn't do anything. But as I got out of the car, I could clearly see what he felt: relief. It was the first time my dad was able to get me to stay in one place for more than two or three nights in a row. He knew I was going to be safe, at least for a little while.

At first, I didn't want to be in treatment. Every night, I would plot how I was going to run away the next day. I was the youngest person there and I felt completely out of place.

One day, we were sitting in group and I was saying how I just wanted to leave.

There was this emo girl sitting across from me, dressed all in black. She sneered, "What do you know? You're perfect." It was funny to me that anyone could think that, but looking back I can sort of see where she was coming from.

The thing is, I looked like a normal teenager whose biggest thrill would have been sneaking into the R-rated film or taking a sip of beer. In the same way that my parents always looked perfect from the outside, I tried to look the part too. Even in my wildest days I had a fairly preppy style, and I'm sure that if I was off drugs and eating, sleeping and showering on a normal schedule, I could have easily passed for a girl who had it all. My innocence had certainly protected me but it was also a mirage. Because I was so broken within, I didn't think I could ever be fixed.

The emo girl and I ended up being friends but I realized then that in so many ways, not much had changed from when we were kids and everything looked so perfect and normal on the outside, even if we were falling apart on the inside.

I stayed at the rehab center for almost two months and when I left, I went home to my dad's and I stayed clean for almost a year. I tried my hand at being a normal 15-year-old girl, thinking about 15-year-old girl stuff. But my past, and my family's past, wasn't something I could escape.

I turned 16 and finally started to face that my father's legal troubles still weren't over. After years of appeals they were taking my father to trial again. In so many ways, I had been avoiding the reality of my mother's death but I was also avoiding this—the collateral damage from her death.

There was one former employee who had told the cops that my father had asked him jokingly if he had a gun, in reference to my mom. Because of that, the charges became more serious, and he was facing harsher penalties.

I can still hear how my dad made the joke, like, *God, this woman.* Not like, *God I want to kill this woman.* But that was all it took. My dad knew his best option was to take a plea bargain, again not wanting to put us through the trauma of more trials. He was sentenced to five years in prison. They tried to appeal it but it seemed like there was no way my dad was going to walk away from that night without serving time. The judge who sentenced him was a well-known women's rights activist. She could have given my dad even more time, but in the end actually sentenced him to less time than the mandatory minimum. It was clear even to her how truly devastated my dad was over what had happened.

During all of this, I came home and enrolled in the local high school. I had three months sobriety and no education since the sixth grade. Now that I was in this big traditional high school, it felt more surreal than the acid trip that landed me in treatment in the first place. After shooting drugs on the streets for years, I just couldn't get into passing notes or going to the basketball game. I couldn't relate to the kids there and they certainly couldn't relate to me. It had nothing to do with being "smart" or "stupid": I was smart (I like to think I still am) and whenever I bothered to engage with schoolwork, I usually got good grades without having to try very hard. It was more that my life had changed so much in such a short period of time that being in school, surrounded by "normal" kids, felt like someone else's life. I told my dad I couldn't do it.

"But honey, you're doing so good," my dad said, looking like he had aged a hundred years in less than three.

"I just can't do that school," I explained. I had actually been feeling pretty good sober. I liked waking up in my own bed every day, and now that Shelby was almost four, I liked coming home from school and playing with her. I loved being with my younger sisters. It was almost like I needed that time away to accept the fact that my mom was no longer there. Jezi was long out of the house and I was the eldest sister now. It felt good to be a part of my family again.

My dad and I decided it would be better if I went to an alternative school and he found me one in the area. On my first day of school, I knew I was home.

Alternative schools were made for kids like me—kids who had dropped out, used drugs, been to treatment, been to juvie. I wasn't some outlier but right in the middle of the group.

I made a close circle of friends, particularly a boy whose mother had also died, but from natural causes.

While at school, I also met my first boyfriend. He was 21, and I was in love with him, which meant I was devastated when he broke up with me suddenly. Once again, I felt like I had been suddenly cut adrift. I told my new best friend, "I'm going back on the streets."

I didn't just *end up* back on the streets. I made the clear and conscious decision to return. I will never forget the look of hurt on my friend's face when I told him. Years later I ran into him again, and I could tell from the way he acted that that wound had never quite healed.

When my dad was waiting to go to prison, I went back to using. I called Taryn, who had never gotten sober, and hooked back up with her. She had a new boyfriend named Manny, a 25-year-old drug dealer. Though we had been shooting drugs on the streets for years, we believed that we were now finally adults. No one had any right to tell us what to do. We didn't need to hide our choices or our lives. We were 16.

One night, we were at Manny's house when a friend of his named Dave came over. I thought he looked like Colin Farrell. I was instantly obsessed.

Before treatment, I hadn't really paid much attention to guys; I was just focused on the drugs. But now I was older and had been clear-headed enough to meet boys, to flirt with them and to want a boyfriend myself.

I can't help but laugh at how love blinds. He was twice my age! But he was my first love and at that point I was sure we'd be together forever. We would use and party together. I was still living at home and we would crash in a shed out back. I didn't think about the fact that Dave must have been one messed up guy if the best place he could find to sleep was a shed in his teenage girlfriend's backyard.

My dad was still at the house awaiting his sentencing, as the process was drawn out over months. Before he was sentenced, we decided to go on a family vacation to Vegas. I convinced my dad that Dave could housesit while we were gone because I didn't want him sleeping somewhere else.

By day two of the trip, Dave was hissing at me over the phone that I better come home.

"I know you're fucking someone!" he yelled at me.

"What? Dave, no," I defended myself, knowing that I would never do that. I might have been a druggie but I was loyal.

"I fucking know you, Sarah. You're a fucking slut! Who is that? Are you sucking some guy's dick right now? I can hear someone's dick."

I was staying in a hotel room with my father, grandmother and four sisters, so the idea of me sucking someone's dick was impossible. And how can you hear a dick anyway? I started to laugh.

"Are you fucking laughing at me, Sarah? Are you fucking laughing? You better not come back here or I'll fucking kill you."

Okay, so if this was a movie and I was your narrator, this is the part where I would stop the film and say, I know. I should have left then and there and never gone back to him.

But as we all know, there is no drug more powerful than love. And at that time, I believed I loved Dave.

When we returned to our house, it had been destroyed. Dave had ripped the stereo out of my sister's car and in the short week we were in Vegas, had started running a meth lab out of my dad's house.

I had only been home a few hours when Dave continued his accusations. We were back in the shed while my dad tried to figure out what to do with us.

"So be honest," Dave said. "Whose dick did you suck?"

I started laughing again at the ridiculousness of it all, finally spitting on the floor in front of him. I joked, "Oh sorry, that must be the cum in my throat." Because honestly, I thought it was funny and I had a smart mouth.

I didn't even see it coming. Dave lunged at me, boxing me with both fists on each side of my head. I could hear the world ringing.

It was the first time he had ever hit me. It was the first time I had ever been hit at all. Even in all my years of using, no one had punched me or kicked me or even pulled my hair. Later, I could see how much this moment really changed me. When I thought I was being annoying, or even just too open, too much like myself, I'd clam up, sure that someone was going to punish me for it.

My father, finally fed up, kicked Dave out—and I

went with him. We ended up living in a junkyard shanty where his friend was running a meth lab, a downgrade even from my dad's shed. By then, the abuse had become habitual. It's another one of those freeze-frame moments: I was just a kid. I should have been living at home with my family, going to school and thinking about my future. Instead I had tied myself to a violent person and a violent life, one in which my safety was often the last thing on my mind.

The thing was, when Dave hit me, I always fought back. I had my mother's spirit in me, after all. I knew, objectively, that Dave hitting me was wrong, I was also still me—aka the kind of person who can't help but fight and talk back even when I know I probably shouldn't. There was one instance where Dave had me curled up in a ball, because he knew I was trying to gouge his eyes out. And the only thing I could do was scratch him with—literally—the one finger I had managed to get loose. He had every part of me held down, but I was still trying to fight back—with one fingernail! But it didn't matter because Dave would take it to the next level, punching me in the face until I couldn't see out of either eye. He would beat me in front of our friends. Taryn still remembers a time I was on the floor and he was kicking me in the stomach with steel-toed boots. She thought I was going to die but she didn't know what to do. Dave was a scary dude.

The fights usually started over the same things:

Dave accusing me of cheating on him or stealing from him, things I later realized *he* was doing and then reversing the accusation onto me. I would run away to go home from time to time so I could sleep in a warm room and heal from the bruises. I learned to cover them with makeup so no one would see, though I can't imagine my family didn't know. One day, my dad saw a residual bruise on my cheek.

"Sarah, you don't have to go back to him," he said. "You can stay here. You can come home."

I nodded but I knew that just like I had to go back to the drugs, I had to go back to Dave.

I returned to the junkyard and within the next month, I started feeling sick. I would wake up vomiting in the morning. I knew what was going on before I wanted to admit it to myself, but finally I got a test at the drugstore and confirmed it: I was 16 years old and pregnant.

Around the same time, in mid-2000, my father was sentenced to five years, finally heading into prison just as I was preparing to have my first child. I wish I could say Dave and I followed in my father and mother's early footsteps, getting sober and cleaning up our act. But we spent most of the pregnancy in that junkyard, cooking and smoking meth as my belly grew.

And then Dave was arrested too, on an outstanding drug charge. I went home for a few months. I was 16 but I decided I was going to do right by this baby. I was going to grow up and take care of him. I found out I was having a boy and that made it feel more real. I wondered what he would look like and what his personality would be.

I was going to name him Joshua and I couldn't wait to be his mommy.

I got my GED and tried to find a job. I even saved up enough in that short time to get a car. It wasn't so different than when I had gotten sober two years before. I cleaned up, made friends, started living a normal life—well, as normal as it gets for a pregnant 16 year old. But I was excited about what was going to happen next.

And then they let Dave out of jail. Within a week, he stole my car while I was at work. I lost that job a week later and by the end of the month, I was back to living with Dave, using drugs and getting beat up so regularly that I didn't even notice anymore.

"Who gave you that car?" Dave accused me one night, convinced I couldn't have bought it on my own.

"No one, Dave," I tried to reason with him. "I bought it myself."

"Not a chance. And no way your stupid daddy bought it now that he's in prison."

The problem was, once Dave got an idea in his head, he couldn't let go of it. He would beat me until I would surrender, saying that I had fucked someone else or agreeing with whatever other delusion he had.

But that night, it didn't matter what I said. He aimed his steel-toed boot right at Joshua.

After he left the room, I knew something was wrong but I was afraid to go to the hospital. By the time I made it there, I was in full-fledged labor. Josh was only 32 weeks old.

They ended up having to do an emergency C-section. They let me hold my baby afterwards but then CPS came in and told me that I couldn't take him home. It had been clear upon my arrival that I was high. Dave came to the hospital once and saw the baby in the NICU but wouldn't see him again for two years.

CPS explained that I wasn't allowed to take my baby and that unless I had family to provide for him, he would be placed in foster care until I was able to take care of him myself. I nodded, trying to pretend it was better this way. I couldn't have the baby around someone as violent as Dave. The social workers tried to tell me that it wasn't safe for me to stay with the baby's father either but I couldn't hear them. I just wanted to get back home.

I worried about what Dave would be doing while I was in the hospital. We were managing to live in a small studio apartment, selling little bags of meth when we didn't use it all. I imagined Dave fucking some woman in our bed and though I loved my baby, I was too fucked up to be able to choose Josh over his father. I couldn't even think about what my life would look like if it were just the two of us, Josh and me, trying to make it without Dave.

I know it's not an easy thing to understand unless you have lived in that kind of relationship. The abuse was the bond. I lived in fear and yet some sort of awe. Dave was my drug. Since the minute my mom died, I had been determined to self-destruct and here he was —someone who was willing to destroy me.

I wouldn't have known what to do with real love, the kind that doesn't involve doing drugs for days at a time or getting punched in the face for looking at someone the wrong way. When I was sober, I couldn't wait to hold my baby but now the thought made me shudder. I knew they were going to take him one day anyway. It was better that it was now, before he saw too much or got hurt himself.

I called my grandmother out of the hope that she would take Joshua, but her husband didn't want to take in a newborn. Joshua went into foster care and I went home to Dave.

Joshua was living with a sweet woman who hadn't been able to have children. She had been waiting for a gift like that for a long time. I began to meet up with the two of them for visits, and I could see the fear in her eyes. I was getting better, which meant Joshua would likely go home. My grandmother's husband had passed away and when Joshua was six months old, the courts gave her custody while I completed my outpatient program.

During this time, Dave went to jail again—for a whole year. And I was free. CPS had stayed in touch with me and explained that I could go to a treatment program and they would help me.

I went to that program, I believed I would finally get the break I needed. I moved into a homeless shelter for domestic violence victims and even though Dave was still out there, I felt safe.

I was living with my grandmother and Joshua, and I was finally getting to be the mom I had dreamt of being. Dave was behind bars, and for the first time since I was six years old, life felt peaceful. I got a little job, took care of Joshua, went to my recovery meetings and visited my dad in prison so he could meet his grandson.

It felt like my last 10 years had been filled with pain and death and violence. And now, here was this new baby, this new chance at life. And I was going to be okay.

3

HITTING ROCK BOTTOM
WHERE AT LEAST THE FOUNDATION IS SOLID

When Josh turned one, Dave was released from prison. I wish I could say I ignored his phone calls, that I notified the police, that I got a restraining order and refused to see him, but I was already so deep into my pattern, I didn't know how to get out. One step forward, 10 steps back. I would get my shit together, begin to rebuild my life, show up for my son and my family—and everyone would begin to think that I was healed.

And then the peace was once again destroyed.

Dave came around, acting like he wanted to see his son. The only time he had ever met his child was when Joshua was in the NICU. How could I deny him?

Within the month I was back with him, smoking meth. I never called my grandmother to let her know I wasn't coming back. I just disappeared. I would get high with Dave and think of the sweet woman who wanted to adopt Joshua. I don't know what made me feel worse—that I had abandoned Joshua or that I had showed up for just long enough to take him away from the woman who could have raised him. My grandmother threatened to call CPS but by that time, she had gotten too close with Joshua to let him go. I was 17 when he was born. Now, I was just barely 18. During the times when I did see Josh, I started to feel more like his sister than his mother.

My grandmother continued to care for him as I found myself caught in the same cycle with Dave as I had been before. We were cooking meth, getting high, getting into fights and I would wake up the next morning, unable to see out of one or both eyes, using drugs to ignore the pain.

And then I got pregnant again. I knew this was my chance. I didn't want to get Dave arrested again just to buy my freedom. This time I was walking away on my own. I had to get out of there but the thought was terrifying. Every time I would try to leave, he would threaten me and I would go back, convinced it was the only thing I could do. CPS was watching me and they would call me when I went back to him, telling me what was going to happen with my current pregnancy if I didn't get clean and get away.

The cops tried to help me too. They had seen this

situation many times before, and they would try to convince me that I could leave.

One cop looked me in the eye, compassionate but tired of showing up because the neighbors had complained again that it sounded like I was being murdered. "Honey," he said, "he doesn't care about you. He's going to hurt you real bad one of these days or worse. You walk out now or you might not ever be walking out of here."

I heard him speaking but I couldn't hear the words. I knew what he wanted me to do, what I wanted to do, but I just couldn't do it.

Finally, I found us a little apartment and I tried to convince myself that we could do this. Dave was using, but I was trying to stay sober. I hoped we could start again. Dave could still be suspicious and angry but the big fights lessened. Then I realized Dave was using again and I couldn't take it. I imagined him getting high with other women while I was pregnant and alone.

Knowing that CPS was on to me, I came up with the idea that I should get out of their reach and have the baby in Idaho, so I ran—while I was in active labor. As you can imagine, I didn't get very far. After I gave birth to Jacob, he too was taken and placed in foster care. Again, my grandmother said she couldn't take him, that one was more than enough—but as soon as she saw Jacob, she changed her mind and took him in.

Once Jacob was with my grandmother, I knew he was safe. My grandmother once again had to fight CPS for the chance to take him in—she was already in her 60s, and they didn't want to give her yet another baby.

It's hard to express what giving up my kids felt like. Looking back, it's hard to believe I let it happen. I've always loved kids and babies, and the fantasy of being a mom and raising amazing, adorable kids was something that had been with me since I was a little girl.

Life was no different back with Dave. If anything, it had become more violent. Dave blamed me for losing Jacob and started spending more time out of the house. I knew he was sleeping with someone else.

I started cooking dope on my own and things began to get really dark. One day, I came home to find Dave asleep, and I dug in his pockets—only to find a love letter from another woman.

I knew that my friend's boyfriend had a gun. I took off for their apartment and convinced my friend that I needed to borrow it. I had been smoking so much meth that I was in a full psychosis. I took the gun to a party and pulled it out.

"Does anyone know how to use this?" I asked, as people watched in silent fear. "Can someone show me how to use this?"

Someone there knew Dave and called him, saying that I was threatening to kill someone. Dave tracked me down and as soon as I pulled out the gun, he tackled me and took it away. There isn't much I am grateful to Dave for, but had I killed him that night, I would have been writing a very different story.

Not long after, Dave got picked up and was sentenced to five years. Both my boys were at my grandmother's and I knew that she was now their mother. I had no reason to go back there. I had no reason to get sober. Instead, I started my own run—cooking meth, selling drugs, stealing from stores across Washington and Idaho.

It was a warm Wednesday in May when I entered the Macy's in Coeur d'Alene. I was planning to hit the jewelry department, lift what I needed and get out. But the security team caught me and when the cops came, they searched my car, finding other stolen items and some meth. Unlike weed, meth isn't the kind of thing cops occasionally let slide, and I knew I was about to be in a new kind of trouble.

For the first time, I was the one put in handcuffs and led away. Though I had been arrested before, it was always for misdemeanors—possession charges or domestic assault with Dave. But this time was different. They charged me with a crime spree, a felony charge. Idaho was demanding that I get a minimum sentence. I ended up getting five years, like my dad and like Dave. Luckily, I was assigned to a DOSA program, which is the Drug Offender Sentencing Alternative. This allows drug offenders to complete substance use treatment and get reduced time. I pled to four years and ended up doing 18 months. Eight of those months were in county, which was hard time. Because people aren't meant to be in county jails longer than a few months, they don't have the same kind of regimented, routine stability that exists in prison. There are usually fewer (if any) programs, and most people are just focused on getting out and right back to the lives they were living before. In county, you're locked down 23 hours a day, and in the Pacific Northwest, that means you might not see the sun for the entirety of your stay. Also, the food sucks.

Once I moved to state, though, it got easier. I knew it was only a matter of time before I got out, and once again, I had big plans. I was sober the entire time I was in and I became committed to the idea of getting my boys back. My grandmother would bring them to visit me in prison and though Jacob was barely one and Joshua was three, I knew they could tell I wasn't in a good place. They wanted me home too. By now, my dad was also home. He got out with good time and had returned to the carpet store and his old life. My sisters were still living at his house too. There was so much for me to return to.

In prison, I became good friends with my cellie Jennifer, a girl I had known in Spokane. She was part of a famous crime family that everyone knew to be crazy. Her dad was from the South and spoke with a deep drawl. They had all moved into the Spokane Valley and basically took it over, running drugs and who knows what else. They weren't the friendly drug buddy types. They were crazy and they were ruthless. But when Jennifer showed me a picture of her brother Teddy, I could tell he was different.

When I got out, I met him and we immediately started dating, even though I soon realized I wasn't attracted to him.

Teddy *was* different, though. He was sweet and emotional and would cry all the time. He worshipped me. After years of being beaten and humiliated, it felt nice to be treated like a princess. Even if my prince was a drug user with a crazy crime family, and even if I wasn't really in love with him.

After 18 months of being sober, I started using again with Teddy, except now I was also running my own drug business, which was a lot more professional than the shit I pulled with Dave. As far back as I can remember, I've had an interest not just in having money, but in making it. If I got a paycheck, the first thing I'd think would be "how can I turn this into even more money?" And honestly, I was good at selling drugs, especially as a cute, young girl who didn't seem like a threat. But moving drugs meant being around drugs pretty much 24/7. It was a recipe for disaster. I mean, what would really be shocking is if I had been around all those drugs and *not* started doing them again, you know?

For some reason, in the midst of all this craziness, he decided we should get married. I knew I didn't love Teddy. I wasn't even attracted to him. But somehow I felt like I had no other choice. At least he was nice to me. That alone made him marriage material, right? We had a courtroom wedding and then went back to using and running drugs.

Our house got raided, and we got arrested. Lucky enough to get bailed out, we came home and I tried to stay sober. I wanted to fight the charges, especially since they wanted to make me out to be some massive drug kingpin. But one day, I woke up sick and I knew exactly what was wrong. I didn't need anyone to tell me I was pregnant again. But this time, I knew I wouldn't keep it. I had already lost two children and I knew there was no way my grandmother could take a third. Jacob was already showing signs of behavioral issues. And I knew I was a lost cause. Sure, maybe I would get some sober time under my belt—I could stay sober for a few months while pregnant, maybe while I was in prison—but once I was out on the streets, all bets were off.

Then the system made the decision for me. I ate a poppyseed muffin, and my scheduled drug test came back positive, even though I told them beforehand about the damn muffin. The prosecutor must have hated me, because she immediately revoked my bail. I was already 8 weeks pregnant. As soon as I was arrested, I told them I was pregnant and requested abortion services.

However, first I had to be booked, arraigned, negotiate my plea, get sentenced and then processed. By the time I made it to the medical side of the county hospital with my left hand gripping the stretcher and my right handcuffed on the other side, I was 20 weeks pregnant and facing another year in. Miraculously, they let me participate in the DOSA program again.

But after I emerged from the abortion, I was determined that this time I would do it right. It felt like a completely different experience than when I was in prison the previous time. Instead of making plans to hook up with my cellie's brother when I got out, I started reading books and dreaming about a different future. I didn't want to have lost the baby in vain. This stint in prison, however long it was going to last, had to mean something.

The first time I went to prison, it had been expected. I was on a full-tilt psychotic run. Just like my mom, it was only a matter of time before I hit the wall. At least I wasn't waking up with both eyes swollen shut. And though I was in no place to take the boys back, I was sober some of the time, able to show up for family dinners and things.

Now, I was back in prison. Even at my worst, I

always felt like I had been in charge of my own destiny. When I left the alternative school and headed back to the streets, I chose to go there. Even all the times I returned to Dave, I knew what I was doing. A part of me hoped he would kill me, believing that it would make things easier for all of us.

But I didn't make this decision and for the first time in my life, I felt out of control. I had started to get some life back and now I didn't want to lose it. For the first time, I really wanted to get better. I started to dissect my thought process, going through the reasons for all my decisions:

Why did I leave home when I was 12?

Why did I return to the streets?

Why did I stay with Dave?

Why did I give up the boys?

Why did I marry Teddy?

Why did I terminate the pregnancy?

Why did I end up back in prison?

After years of believing that I knew what I was doing and thinking that, despite all the evidence to the contrary I could trust my gut, I realized I couldn't trust myself at all. I knew that I didn't want to get out of prison only to have an ordinary life. Plus, when you have a felony on your record, good luck getting a 9-5 job in corporate America. And I knew I didn't just want to end up at Walmart, barely making enough money to survive, bagging people's groceries when I knew I could do so much more.

Was I just going to get some job, make minimum wage, work until I retired and then die? Was that worth getting sober and staying clean for? If I was going to stay off drugs, I was going to have to find something *better than drugs*. I didn't know what I was going to do when I got out but I began to believe it was going to be something extraordinary.

I realized that it doesn't matter what your prison looks like. Many of us live in the 10-foot cell of our own limiting beliefs. We don't realize how much we allow ourselves to be boxed in by what happens to us in our lives. We live in trauma like it's a cage, blaming our childhoods for the locked doors when we are holding the key the entire time. I began to see that the key was in my hand—I just had to do something with it.

I started hanging out in the prison library, and I'll say this: if you're serving time right now, the people who spend the most time in the library are the ones most likely to get out. They're also the ones least likely to come back.

Why? Because they're curious. And curious people realize that there is so much more to discover than prison or the shit that landed you there. Reading even one book, going to one meeting or making one real friend who has the same goals you do is one small investment in your future. It's a promise to yourself that you're going to keep turning the page, that you're going to wake up tomorrow to find out where the story goes next. I had hit rock bottom but I also found a solid foundation down there. I started reading Tony Robbins and whatever personal development books I could find. Deepak Chopra, Dr. Phil, Marianne Williamson—I was determined to find the key. The other ladies would laugh and call me Oprah.

The thing about prison is that time slows down so much. Now, I barely have time to read an article on my phone before I fall asleep at night but in prison, all you have is time. And this round, I wasn't wasting mine. I was 22 years old and I had two children waiting for me on the outside. Even my father, after he came to visit one weekend with the boys and my grandmother, remarked, "You've never looked this good, Sarah." I could see on their faces and hear in their voices that as hard as it had been for them to watch me struggle, I might actually be making some real progress. I also started really writing for the first time. Every day I would make lists about my future: things I was going to do, places I was going to go. Sometimes I'd even sketch outfits I dreamed of wearing. Years later, I managed to actually wear those outfits. Later, I'd come to recognize this as my first real experience with making vision boards, with committing to the idea that by speaking or writing it down, you can make it happen.

I had never felt better either. After years of being

near-dead or pretending to be dead, I felt completely alive. I knew that this aliveness was going to save me on the outside. I needed to have radical hope because the boring, commonplace hope wasn't going to save me out there. Believing that my life could be extraordinary might just sustain me. I wanted to give back. I wanted to make it right. And I wanted to get out of prison, finally in one piece.

I knew that as soon as I was out of prison, time was going to fly by, so I tried to relish my time inside. How often in life do we get the chance to be so alone with ourselves, to focus on our thoughts, feelings and dreams? I certainly don't want to make prison sound like some kind of health spa, but for me it was probably the first time I'd ever really had to think about Sarah and what she might want, what she might be able to do. I was thirsty for change and I spent every day drinking from the fountain of knowledge. I would pray to God at night: "God, if you give me a great life, I will give it back and make it right." And I began to believe that something amazing was going to happen when I got out of prison.

You know those studies where they test a group of people and tell them that they have exceptional aptitude? Previously, the group thought they had average intelligence, maybe even a little less than average. But now, they're told that they're basically geniuses. And you know what they go out and do? They do extraordinary things. Because they believe they are extraordinary, and belief is enough.

Just by telling ourselves that we're amazing, we suddenly start doing amazing things. Belief is a powerful current; it can be used to light us up or short us out. But I began using it to prepare myself for the release. And that day was quickly approaching.

I know for a lot of people a prison sentence feels just like that—a prison sentence—but most people who wind up in prison are just projects waiting to happen. We're broken, and we can go to prison and deepen the brokenness or we can see it as an opportunity to heal. We can take advantage of the psychological services, the recovery services, the educational services. The chance to get and stay sober, the way it takes us out of our environments and forces us, for better or for worse, to break patterns and end relationships. We can start looking at prison as the great test. The universe is giving us a time out. We can either change the way we're playing the game so we can start winning or we can get back in there and continue to lose.

I was done losing. I had lost so much to drugs and addiction. I had lost my mother. My father. My sons. Myself. I had lost the last 10 years of my life, swallowed in a cloud of meth smoke and violence and fear and the belief that I was better off dead. And while some of those things I'll never get back, others weren't lost forever. I just had to be ready to find them.

The day my grandma picked me up from prison, I knew two things: I was going to do it differently this time and I was going to divorce Teddy.

As we drove home on a rainy February day, almost two years after the date of my arrest and my abortion, I looked over at my now older dad. We had been through so much. We had lost so many of the same things. I flashed back to two years earlier when he was sitting on my bed, pleading for me to stay home, to get better.

I didn't go back to my grandmother's this time. I knew that she was now raising the boys as her own and though they knew that I was technically their mother, I would just be throwing another wrench into their lives if I showed up now, when mine was still such a mess. Instead, I went back to the room where my dad had sat on my bed. Shelby and Luci were still living there. Jezi was living with her boyfriend and had a kid. Courtney was living in Vegas, constantly partying.

I remember going to the bathroom that first night home, before going to bed. I washed my face and as I was drying it, I looked hard at myself in the mirror. It felt like I was looking at myself for the first time, at the grown up I had so quickly become. And I knew that the only way to go was up.

4

BELIEVING IN YOURSELF
TAKES A WHOLE LOT OF TIME, WORK AND ENERGY

This is the crossroads. The moment when you move forward into an unknown but hopeful future or where you retreat back into the way that things have been. Years later, I would read about how the nerves in your brain actually create a path based on the habits you form. It's like a marble rolling down a well-worn track. Sure, you can get it out of its groove but it takes a shock to the system to bounce it from its place, and a whole new set of habits to create a new groove.

I needed a new groove but I didn't even know how to start. All I knew was that I had to get up and not get high. All I knew was that my old way of living life didn't work. So I decided I would just start doing the opposite of what my gut told me to do. If it told me to call Teddy, I wouldn't pick up the phone. If it told me to lay in bed all day, I would get up. I would live in whatever way was the opposite of my old patterns.

I knew that getting a job was key. I had to get moving and I had to get busy or it wouldn't be long before I would pick up that phone and call my old life again.

I had served almost two years and was lucky to be free. When I got arrested the second time, I hadn't even finished my first term with DOSA after failing to complete the mandated drug program. And I had to complete DOSA or I would be back in.

I didn't have a choice. It was use and go back to prison or stay sober. And while I had used my prison time to lay the groundwork for my future, it wasn't a place I had any desire to return to. At that point, I had been sober for over two years so the groove had gotten more comfortable. Now, I just needed to keep it that way.

Before I had gone to prison, I had been working in a coffee stand (that's where I had eaten the infamous poppyseed muffin). It was in a dusty parking lot, a spot people would swing by on their way to work in the morning. I was the morning barista. I had no experience, I was just out of prison and I was broken in ways I hadn't allowed myself to feel in years. But every morning, I got up at 4 am and drove to the coffee stand. I learned how to make coffees and be kind to customers.

One of those customers was a guy named Seevu. Seevu was from Laos and had worked in Child Protection Services. We became friendly and after a few months, he told me that he wanted to open a coffee stand himself, and that if I could find one, he would allow me to run it. I never expected anyone to be so kind to me. I had been living for years in a world where people didn't help unless they wanted something from you. But Seevu didn't want anything. I got to know his wife and family, and in a way, they showed me what I could be. I could own a business, get married (for real), have a family. I could have a stable home, one where we ate dinner together every night and talked about our days. I could become the kind of person who took care not just of her own family, but of her community. And maybe if I did that, other people might look at me and think that they could do it too. I also know now that Seevu wasn't just being kind. He wasn't offering me a handout. He saw that I was a good, hard worker, and he knew I had potential to stretch and grow at work. And later, when we talked about our lives, I learned that Seevu recognized a kindness in me too. As an immigrant, he'd faced racism, prejudice and the hardships that come with trying to learn a new culture and a new way of life. By being friendly, I'd shown him something he needed to see as well.

But first, I had to get a divorce. Teddy was still chasing me around town, hoping things would work out between us, and I knew it was time to explain why I left him.

We met for coffee, and I told Teddy that he was one of my best friends but that I didn't want to be married anymore. I wanted more for myself, even if I didn't know exactly what it was going to look like yet. Once upon a time, the fact that Teddy didn't hit me was enough to make me think he'd be a good husband. But after having done time in prison and committed myself to something new—something hopeful—I knew I deserved more.

I could tell he was heartbroken. Teddy might have come from a violent, insane family, but he was the outlier. For a months, he continued to follow me around but I was always focusing on something else. I was going to build Seevu's business. I had told Seevu everything—my past time, my struggles. I worried that being so honest might cost me this opportunity, but I also knew that *not* being honest wasn't the way I wanted to be with him. I wanted to show him that I had integrity, that I had motivation, and I wanted to show myself those things too. Having a job—a purpose—can be such a light in the dark for so many people and it's why I work so hard to be a good boss for the employees I have now.

I did well in my new management position, except that the coffee stand only did business in the morning, which meant I would work two-hour shifts and only make $20. Finally, I went to Seevu and asked if I could work more hours. He told me that he was planning to sell the coffee stand and asked if I wanted to buy it. He said he would sell me the business for $1 but the equipment would cost $20,000.

When my mom died, she left enough for each of us to get $25,000 on our 25th birthday. It felt like another divine moment—it was the almost exact amout Seevu had offered to sell me the business for, and he had no idea. I was a year away from receiving my inheritance but I felt like I was so close to it that my dad might be willing to loan me the money. He would be taking a chance: I had been in and out of treatment and jail, and he had no guarantee that I was actually going to get it together and make this work. But my dad has always instilled a kind of hustle in me, and I think he must have known on some level that I was really ready to try.

Whenever I speak with women coming out of prison, I tell them that they've all already been entrepreneurs. Being a hustler is entrepreneurship. Whether you've been selling drugs or even sex, whether you've been shoplifting and running to the pawn stores—you've been buying and selling, negotiating and marketing. On the streets, getting what you need to survive each day is a series of business deals. Once you have a felony, the options can be limited but you can always run your own business. I know that it isn't easy to build something from the ground up. But cooking meth isn't easy either. Getting thrown down a staircase isn't easy. Having children removed from your care isn't easy. Going to prison is not easy.

Just because you think something isn't easy doesn't make it impossible.

We often accept the worst outcomes, forgetting how hard they are, when we can make real progress in our lives. It's all about getting out of that old groove.

I wanted out of that old groove for good. It didn't matter that I didn't know what I was doing. And trust me, I had no clue. I just believed that the coffee stand was going to be the answer. I was going to figure it out and make it happen, hustling just like I had been since the age of 12, when I ran away from home. I told my dad about the coffee shop.

"Is this really want you want to do, Sarah?" he asked.

"I do," I explained. "And this is just the first one; I could buy more and grow the business. I love being at the shop." Once I envisioned myself as the owner of one coffee shop, envisioning myself as the owner of a coffee shop empire came easily. If I could run one, why couldn't I run 10? Why couldn't this be just the beginning for me?

"Running your own business takes a lot of time," my dad warned.

"I've got time," I replied. And I did. For the first

time in my life, I had a wide road in front of me and I knew I was going to get where I was going. My dad agreed to loan me the money and at the age of 24, Blissful Blends became mine.

Again, it wasn't easy. I had no idea what I was doing. I had an employee who was only about two years younger than me.

Though I could barely afford to, I kept her shift so that I could focus on figuring out how to run the business. I had to learn how to pay taxes and watch my cash flow. I had to figure out how to budget and buy supplies, how to negotiate costs and get things cheaper. I had to learn how to structure pricing so that I wasn't giving away inventory, how to figure out the formula to get the best profit margin out of each drink while still keeping the customer happy. And I had to learn how to deal with customers who weren't happy, and how to keep them coming back anyway. I had to start taking ownership not just of the business but also my life.

And that life was starting to get more interesting. One, because I met someone who would change it forever. And two, because once again, I had started using.

Part of my "do the opposite of what you think you should" plan was to date people who I didn't think I liked. For years, I went for guys who looked like they could hurt you. I decided I would say yes to someone

Believing in Yourself | 53

who wasn't like the other guys in my life. There was a guy who came into the coffee shop a lot who was nice but not my type. And then one day, he gave me his number.

"Are you sure?" I asked him, handing him his quad latte, our signature drink.

"Umm," he looked around, confused by my question. "You don't have to call me."

I hesitated but a voice in my head reminded me: do the opposite.

"Okay," I said.

I did actually work up the nerve to call him but got the wrong number.

He came in again and I mentioned that I'd tried to call, and he figured out that I hadn't misdialed—he'd written down the wrong phone number.

At this point, I wasn't sure if the universe was playing tricks or if it was just trying to trick me into liking this guy. I grabbed his hand and wrote my number on his arm.

He called me later that day and a few days after, we went out to dinner. I remember thinking he just looked too clean. Though he worked construction, his clothes were clean, his hair was nice, and when he told me he liked the band Maroon 5, I thought I might be a little too rough around the edges for him.

I just wasn't used to normal men. I was used to guys who did time and cooked meth.

But the other big surprise was how well we got along.

I didn't lie about my past. I told him about going to prison and how I was trying to change my life. The old me might have lied, or at least omitted some of the more hair-raising parts of my story. But the new me was one that understood that the old me was a part of my life too.

Then I laughed and said, "So I'm going to guess this will be our last date."

"Why?" he asked innocently.

"I mean, if you're not afraid of a felon."

"Should I be afraid?"

I realized it was a good question. Should he? For years, I had been out there surviving. Often I was the victim of abuse but that didn't mean I didn't hurt people. I stole from friends and family. I failed to show up. I had abandoned my own boys. Should he be afraid?

"I don't think so," I said, looking down before glancing back up. His eyes were on me. For a moment, I believed that I could be with someone like him, that I could live a normal life. "I'm doing better."

And I was trying—I had been out of prison for four months. I had started renting my own little apartment and the business, stressful as it was, was progressing. I was spending more time with the boys and my dad.

For the first time in a long time, it felt like I was truly growing.

At the end of the night, Mike asked me out again and as he did, he laughed and said, "And no, I'm not afraid of a felon."

I'd like to say we took it slow. But sometimes when you know, you know. A friend once told me that when you're with the wrong person, there is nothing you can do to get it right, but when you're with the right person, there is nothing you can do to fuck it up.

So I guess that's why I tried to fuck it up.

I was done with my probation and the pee tests but I still didn't know how to disengage from old friends. They were the only ones I had. I actually had become friends with Teddy's new girlfriend and they would sell me drugs. But this time, I thought it was different. I had it under control. I mean, I was running my own business, wasn't I?

I lived the same lie as so many other addicts. It's one thing to know you've got a problem when you're sitting in family or criminal court. But when you have a job—heck, your own freaking business—and everyone is so proud of you, when you overhear your sister on the phone talking about how great you're doing, you begin to believe it. You're doing so great that maybe, you think, a little hit here or a little sniff there won't make that big of a difference. What harm could it really do?

And maybe had I not been dating Mike, it would have been easy to go headfirst into my addiction. But I found it was hard to balance both with him watching.

I would be high and acting crazy, and he'd be like, "Are you okay?"

In a way, his innocence was more motivating than his judgement. He didn't really know what he was dealing with and I felt like all the more of an asshole for it. But it was so hard to let go of those old friends. In part because we had been through so much together and in part because I was 24! I wanted to work, obviously, but I also wanted to live. And though I had the coffee shop, I didn't have a new crowd to hang out with, people to replace the group I had lost, so I kept reaching back out to Teddy and his sister as well as other friends I used with. And like they say, if you keep hanging at the barbershop long enough, you're bound to get a haircut.

One night we were going to a friend's Christmas party and I was doing drugs while I was getting ready. I have no idea how Mike didn't know, but he didn't, though he did get the sense something was up. At the party, I locked myself in the bathroom (after grabbing his phone), and by the time I came out, hours had passed. Mike was angry and confused. One of my friends finally told me that this had gone too far—if I didn't tell him I was using, she would.

Mike's only real question was whether or not I was

going to quit. And quit for good. After so many years, I was worried that I couldn't but also, for the first time in my life, I saw a better life. One where I wasn't dead in the water. One where I was married to Mike, where we could raise the boys together, maybe even have children together. I had the coffee shop. I saw a vision of the life I live today. And I knew that I wanted it.

I nodded my head.

"You sure?" Mike asked.

I wasn't sure but I was going to try to make it happen. Over the next month, I kept using but tried to convince Mike that I was fine. I explained that it was no different from him drinking a beer. The look on his face told me how ridiculous that sounded.

"I have, like, a few beers, Sarah," Mike would argue. "You're fucking shooting meth. There's a difference. And to be honest, I don't really like that version of you. She does scare me."

Maybe that was what I had meant when I asked if he was afraid of a felon. Would I scare him off when he saw me using, because deep down I knew I couldn't quit. But I heard the threat in Mike's voice and I decided maybe it was time to take the plunge into my future, even if the water was cold and I wasn't sure if I was going to be able to swim.

"I'll stop," I promised him. "I really will."

And I did. For the first time in nearly a year, I got clean again. I was probably about a month off drugs when I found myself puking in the toilet one night after dinner. I knew that feeling. I could never forget that feeling.

I went to the pharmacy, got a pregnancy test and showed Mike the results. I didn't know what he was going to say but I knew I couldn't have another abortion. No matter what, I was going to keep this baby, I was going to stay sober and I was going to raise him or her on my own if I had to. But just like before, Mike refused to run.

He was definitely nervous. We had only been dating about nine months and I was only a few weeks clean, and yet, there was something so hopeful about that test. We both felt it.

Instead of what I'd done in previous pregnancies—alternately using, getting clean and getting beaten up—this time, I felt what every woman should feel. I felt loved and supportive, I felt sober and safe.

I don't know that I would have stayed clean without that pregnancy. I was determined to do it right this time. I erased all the old numbers from my phone and stopped returning calls. At first, I thought Mike was trying to take over my life. I believed he was just like Dave, separating me from friends and family just so he could abuse me, but the abuse never came. He liked the friends and family of mine who were healthy and supportive but he wasn't afraid to tell me when someone else was doing me harm.

It was still so hard for me to tell the difference. I had trouble attracting the right kind of people. I was quick to find people's strengths, to see past their obvious flaws. And then for some, it was hard to let go. My sister was still using and I wanted to help her. Taryn was struggling and though we had used together, she was still my best friend. It was easy to let go of the Teddys of the world but could I let go of my sister? Or my best friend?

It took me another 10 years to be able to answer that question but at least I started making progress.

I wish I could have made the same decisions for Joshua and Jacob. I knew that having a baby wasn't enough—it hadn't been in the past—but this time, between the baby and Mike and the business, it was all too much to lose.

I gave birth to Connor and after he was born, Mike and I decided it was time to bring home Jacob and Joshua. They were now four and six respectively and it made sense for them to join our new family. I had three boys and I imagined raising them all together. But sometimes dreams don't come true.

For all of their young lives, my grandmother had been raising them as though they were hers. They knew I was Mommy but my grandma was the one who took care of them day in and day out. She was the one that rocked them to sleep at night, the one who was there when they fell down. They were used to her schedule and her routine. Even at age four, Jacob was struggling with behavioral issues and when he came to our house, those issues exploded.

Mike didn't know how to handle it. He believed they needed a stricter household than the one they were used to at my grandmother's but enforcing rules just caused more trouble. As much as I wanted the boys with us, I realized I had already done enough harm in their lives. They wanted to be at their grandmother's and I didn't want to make things any harder on them.

My grandmother was also distraught over the idea of them living with me. She was older but they were now her sons too. We agreed that they could come and stay with us whenever they wanted but that their primary home would be with my grandmother.

It wasn't an easy decision to make and I worried about whether I would be able to stay sober through it. It felt like I was losing my boys again but I also knew that I could never make it right with them if I was using. I could offer them a safe and loving home whenever they wanted to visit, I could continue to go to their games, show up for their school functions and be a part of their lives in the ways they wanted me to and not in ways that would make it more difficult for them.

It was time for me to take responsibility for everything in my life—my relationship, my parenting and my business (which I was beginning to realize might be bigger than I was capable of managing).

But if I had one thing, it was determination. I wanted to ensure that I could take care of Connor no matter what happened. And I knew that in order to do so, I had to start building Blissful Blends into something more than a one-stop coffee stand.

I was clean, I was a new mother and I was ready for that future that I had envisioned when I first met Mike and began to believe in change.

I was ready.

5

BUILDING A BUSINESS
IS HARD AS FUCK!

So here was my skill set when I took over Blissful Blends. I knew how to cook meth, steal jewelry from department stores and sell drugs (though I was never really good at that last one, which can happen when you're too busy getting high on your own supply). I had never made coffee before, never paid payroll taxes, never used Quickbooks. I'm not even sure I had ever heard of Quickbooks.

I knew how to survive in prison and trade candy for soap. I knew how to cover my face when getting kicked with a steel-toed boot so my head took the bruise and not my face. I knew how to steal Sudafed from behind the pharmacy counter so I could go home and cook.

I did not know how to run a successful, legitimate business.

But I was determined to find out. And once I had

Connor, the stakes were raised. This wasn't just some little gamble. I was using the only money I had to my name; this was my future. I knew I had to start making it work or I was going to spend the rest of my life dependent on a man. I felt like I had felt back in prison, when I started reading every book I could get my hands on, thirsty for change. But this time, I knew the change I wanted was to be successful in business.

I've never wanted to make money for the sake of making money, but for as long as I can remember, making money is what I've wanted to do. Money, to me, represents freedom: the ability to walk out of a bad situation or the ability to invest in something that could pay off down the line. It means the ability to hire babysitters, to send your kids to private school, to pay bills without worrying the checks will clear. And it's funny: for the first half of my life, I was obsessed with freedom, which to me meant doing whatever the hell I wanted. And where did that get me? Locked up—about as opposite from free as you can get. It took being in prison for me to think about ways to be truly free, and when I started to take my business seriously, I knew I was headed in the right direction.

Sometimes in life, it just feels like you're being given the green light. I had made other decisions which felt like one dead end after another, and usually left me smashing my head against a wall, or having someone else smashing it for me.

But not with Blissful Blends. From my first meeting with Seevu, it felt like every door opened for me. He offered me the business just as I was about to receive my inheritance. And then I didn't even realize how good of a spot I had purchased. For the first year or so, I was just getting by, but then I began to see that I was right on one of the major traffic routes for rush hour. All I needed to do was figure out a way to start driving people in.

But then in 2009, there was construction on the road that shut down traffic for months. I was barely making it.

It got so bad that I started applying for other jobs—at UPS and FedEx, anywhere I thought could employ me. The problem was, not only did I not have much job experience but I also still had that good old felony on my record. No matter how many applications I submitted, I got very few interviews and even fewer offers. It would have been hard for someone with my background and lack of experience to get hired even in the best of times, but this was also happening during a recession, where even entry-level retail jobs were seeing thousands of applications for every one opening.

One night I came home exhausted. I was barely making payroll, and I was bringing no money home.

"You don't have to do this," Mike told me over dinner as I fed Connor, so tired I could barely lift the spoon. I would bring Connor to work with me most days, nursing him in the back and setting up his pack n' play behind the counter. There was no way I could afford to have someone else watch him.

Mike kept saying we could get help but I knew it made more sense for me to just give up the business.

"I can take care of us," Mike continued. "And I know you invested in this but maybe you can sell it and get your money back. It is a good location."

That was the part I couldn't let go of. It was a good location. So if I sold it to someone else and they were successful with it, what did that say about me?

I just couldn't give up that easily; I never could. But as I had seen before, there is nothing like rock bottom to help you start building anew.

I reached out to my accountant Brian, who at least knew more than I did about running a business. He was also seeing first-hand what a terrible job I was doing at running my own.

Since the construction was still continuing, Brian suggested that I connect with my landlord and renegotiate the lease. No one else would be willing to take the space with the current conditions.

I made the call. It was terrifying. But what else could I do?

Here is what I learned about running my own business. If I didn't advocate for it, no one else would. I had to be willing to ask the hard questions, believe in it with all my heart and sell it with all my guts. I had to be willing to do more than barely make it. It's so easy to get swept up in anxiety, in imagining the worst-case scenario. But over the course of my life I've faced a lot of worst-case scenarios and asking my landlord to lower the amount of money I was paying for the space wasn't one of them. The worst thing that could happen was that he'd say no. What did I have to lose? I had to figure out how to kill it. And I did that by starting to ask questions.

Roasters would come in to sell me different coffees and I started asking them about other coffee shops, what they did to make themselves successful, how I could start doing the same. I started paying more attention to the money I was spending and then I made that call to the landlord.

It wasn't easy. I told him that because of the construction, I would be out of business in three months. I had been paying $3000 a month in rent at the time, which I now realize is insane. We're talking Spokane here, not Manhattan, not even Seattle. I told him I could only pay $800 or I was going to have to shut down. He knew what would happen if I left. The spot would be empty until the construction ended, which they were saying was going to be six months. I needed my landlord to reduce the rent, but he also needed something from me—the ability to pay any rent at all, which he wouldn't get if I closed down. And if he did manage to get another tenant, what if they defaulted or damaged the space or wrote a bad check? I was his best option when it came to pulling in steady money.

What I learned in that moment was that negotiation all comes down to one trick: be willing to walk away. And don't bluff. Very few people can bluff well, and people will call you on it. You have to know in your heart that you aren't going to stay in a situation that doesn't support you and be willing to leave.

I was prepared to walk away that day, but the landlord surprised me. He agreed to the $800.

"But once construction ends," he explained, "it will go back up to $1200."

"$1200?" I thought. That's way less than $3000.

I agreed. Once again, I turned to my accountant. He had been to the coffee shop many times, as it was on his way to a number of appointments.

He told me, "Look, if you want people to come to shop, you need to put some love into it. Your coffee is good, the location is good, but the shop has to be inviting too."

I had basically left it the way I found it, which was a rough and ready little coffee shop. It didn't look too different from your local donut shop. Again, this wasn't my background. I had no idea how subway tile could change your backdrop, how colored walls versus white walls influenced your market. I just thought you made coffee, you sold it and you were done.

"Start going to your competition," Brian advised me. "See what they're doing. What does their store look like? What are people ordering? Ask them what their most popular drink is. Spend some time figuring out what makes them successful."

So that's what I did. I went to Starbucks, Dutch Brothers and other smaller shops. I started paying attention to what they looked like and how they worked. Whatever their particular style or menu or vibe, these were places people actually wanted to be and enjoyed spending time at. I started caring about my business in a way I never had.

For so many years, I had avoided caring about things because there was so much uncertainty. One minute someone could be there, and the next they could be gone. I had been afraid to love anything, including my own boys. But with Mike and Connor, I had started to trust that you could show up and that people would stay. The same was true with Blissful Blends. Despite my own mismanagement, it refused to leave. I always made just enough to keep it going. And now, it was time to really invest. And it wasn't about money; it was about me.

I picked apart other coffee stands and looked at what worked. I saw that it was about speed and efficiency. If we could tighten up our costs and increase our speed, if we could start selling baked goods and other add-ons, we would not only attract more customers but also increase profits. I began to learn the art of giving deals.

If someone knows they can get a discount—even if it's 50 cents—they will buy, and likely even spend more. I started selling a 24-ounce quad mocha for $4 and it became a hit. I cleaned up the shop, offered baked goods and made it look like a warm and friendly place to get your morning coffee, even to sit and hang out for a while. Connor was still at work with me some days and it added to the environment. This was a family business and people began to feel at home.

I actually started to make money.

And then I started learning about marketing.

I had never done any sort of advertising for the store. The location did a lot of it for me, but I recognized that when we don't have another choice, we become good at whatever we need to do.

I realized that one coffee shop was good, but that people didn't make money with one coffee shop. They made money with expansion. I tried to get a loan and couldn't, partly because it was a hard time for anyone to get a loan. That's when I learned about the idea of buying a business on contract and that ended up being hugely instructive. I thought that to buy a business you had to have tons of cash but the stand in Idaho was being sold on contract—which meant I'd make payments to the owner until eventually it would be mine. That was a lesson for me in taking assets and turning them into...well, into more assets. In finding opportunity in places you'd least expect it.

But after a while, I realized this particular business deal wasn't worth the effort. And that, too, was a lesson learned. There's power in knowing when something isn't right for you. It might seem crazy to give up a business, especially a good business, but by this point I had made so much happen in my life and career that I knew more opportunities would come. Better opportunities. I ended up selling the business, and now I had a little bit more money and a new idea.

There was a woman in town who had bought up a few coffee stands and started hiring young girls in bikinis to staff the shops. The coffee was terrible and the girls weren't too great either. I thought, "I could do that but way better." In practice it was a *little* harder than I expected (more on that later), but I was right. It was another lightbulb moment for me, where I just knew somehow that I was going to do this and I was going to be fucking great at it.

But when I told Mike, he was not on board.

"Girls are going to serve coffee in bikinis?" he asked. "I don't know, Sarah, that just sounds weird to me."

"Not bikinis...more like lingerie."

"Like Hooters?" He still wasn't getting it.

"Yeah, kind of..."

He was doubtful but I had a vision. I knew that it wasn't just about serving coffee but generating interest. Of course, I had no clue just how much interest I was going to generate. The next few months were tense, both at work and at home, as I tried to figure out how to buy another coffee shop and get this new idea off the ground. Because I knew that this was going to be more than just another small business. It was going to be life-changing for me. I just had to get there.

One day when I was chatting with one of my customers, a professional boxer named Fred, he told me he was impressed by the changes I was making around the shop. I told him about my new idea.

"What would you call it?" he asked.

I smiled, having just come up with the name. "XXX Espresso." Short and to the point, just sexy enough to let people know what they were in for.

He laughed. "So you're just looking for an investor, then?"

"Yeah," I explained. "My husband isn't quite on board, but I know I can convince him. I've already found a location." By this point, I knew enough about how the coffee business worked—and how local traffic worked—to know what made a spot lucrative, and I had my eye on a location that I knew would be perfect.

By that point I had gotten used to asking people if

they wanted to invest so it wasn't any different with Fred.

"You interested in investing?" I asked.

He smiled, raising his eyebrows at the proposition. "I just might be."

He told me to pull together a business plan, so I did. And that's when I learned the other side of running a business—you find out just how much you're capable of. I had barely graduated high school. I mean, I took the GED but spent more time out of school than in it. I didn't know algebra or calculus. I hadn't gone to college or taken any financial courses but suddenly I was learning how to calculate projected profit. I was reviewing traffic count and costs and even completed a profit and loss statement. I found out more about the business I was currently running and I became even more convinced about the one I was about to run.

I showed it to Mike one night after dinner, standing over his shoulder as he read. Finally, he looked up and asked, "You did this?"

I nodded, smiling.

"All on your own?"

"Yeah," I told him. "I mean, I checked with Google."

He stood up, pulled me in and said, "Girl, you're amazing."

Afterwards, he told me he still didn't love the idea

of sexy coffee, but after my plan, he had no doubt I would succeed.

Fred was equally impressed and offered to invest $25,000. It was exactly what I needed to get XXX Espresso off the ground. I had just begun to make money with Blissful Blends, but now I needed to bring a whole new level of energy and initiative to XXX. It took me three months after Fred's first investment to secure the location. He was an amazing negotiatior, and we ended up getting the stand for a great price— and then the search for staff began. I was doing interviews every 15 minutes and still couldn't find the right girls. Plenty applied, but I was looking for a specific type. There's a lot of turnover in this business, and I wanted girls I could count on. But I kept at it, slowly building the team that would launch XXX.

By the end of the first year, I had more stands, and a few years after that I was able to buy Fred out of the partnership and in the next few years, I ended buying two more XXX locations, and changed the name to Devil's Brew. The best part about the bikini stands, as we called them, was that every time one would open, the religious groups would try to shut us down, earning us a whole bunch of free media that didn't cost a dime. Moms would show up at city council meetings and give interviews to the local newspaper about how the bikini stands were going to corrupt their kids. Every time that happened, I was right there to remind potential customers that we were open for business. The stores would open with a bang thanks to the people who tried to prevent them.

We ended up having to go to the city council to defend our right to keep them open—and we won, finally putting the argument to rest. As I was building the bikini stands, I was also growing Blissful Blends. After hitting rock bottom, I was now growing stands left and right. One month, I opened two stands at the same time—not something I would recommend, but once I had the formula down, it was just a matter of finding the location and hiring the right staff.

I would usually be at the first shop when it opened at 5 am so Mike would take Connor to school in the morning. I would spend my day going from shop to shop until it was time to pick up Connor, head home for dinner and tally numbers and sales for the day. Within two years, I had two Blissful Blends and three bikini stands. Today, I own 11 coffee stands and Devil's Brew is about to be rebranded as Black Sheep.

Mike likes to joke that I built an empire, but in a way, he's not wrong.

When I got my first coffee stand, I had no clue what I was doing. I didn't understand profit or costs. I didn't understand taxes or traffic. Heck, I didn't even understand interior design. But slowly I built the pieces—the finances, the aesthetic, the marketing—the whole business.

I know that small business is the heart and soul of this country because I have seen it first-hand. We are the ones who learn how to jump into the deep end. And sure, it's freezing at first (not to mention terrifying) but when you have the kind of history I do, you also don't have a lot of choices. If we want to help men and women rehabilitate, truly get them on their feet and leading different lives, we need to offer them paths to entrepreneurship. I know that not everyone has an inheritance at the ready or a father who can help them out. What we need are programs to guide people through the process of building a business—from creating a business plan to getting funding to navigating all the challenges and pitfalls, both the expected and unexpected.

Because what I discovered as the owner of Blissful Blends and Devil's Brew was that a lot of the resourcefulness and determination that served me when I was on the streets were the same skills that helped me to succeed in business. At first, it didn't feel like a natural fit, but over time, I began to see how suited I was for this world.

I wasn't just thirsty for change; I was thirsty for success.

I will never forget when Seevu offered me that first stand and I knew I couldn't let the opportunity pass me by. My impulsivity would override my shyness. But over the last 13 years, succeeding (and also failing) has shown me what I'm made of. Being an entrepreneur not only gave me confidence but also the strength to fail, then get back up and do it again.

Eventually, however, that determination began to take a toll.

I was working nonstop for the dream. I was juggling home life and family life, which included my sisters, who were now struggling with drugs, as well as Joshua and Jacob and the coffee stands. I was running from point A to point B without ever slowing down long enough to check in with the traveler: me.

I was soon burnt out and had little left to give. I was exhausted and knew I couldn't do it anymore. Once again, it was time for a change, and once again, I wasn't sure where to begin.

6

GOING BACK TO BASICS
CAN SOLVE EVERYTHING

By the time I opened my fifth store, I felt like I was dying. Ever since childhood, I'd struggled with my weight. And during my time using, I had picked up an eating disorder that didn't help. I was around 12 or 13, and I was on an acid trip. I had always felt uncomfortable in my own skin—at the age of 12, who doesn't—but during this trip, I had this feeling that I wanted to rip my skin off. I wanted out of my body so badly, I would have been happy to shed my skin right there and leave forever.

The trip ended but that feeling remained. I just wanted to fade away. The next day, I decided I would start starving myself but it wasn't as easy as I expected. I decided I could eat, but only if I threw it up after. This led me on a decades-long battle with bulimia. It amplified my worst fears and ideas, turning the nightmares in my head—of which there were many after my mom died—into reality. Eating disorders are also very much about control. There was so much about my life that was out of control, and throwing up my food was a way I could impose some order on the chaos that threatened to swallow me whole.

Throughout my 20s, I would gain and lose weight, shrinking and swelling with the seasons. When I was in high school, I also started to work out. I realized right away what a high it provided. When I wasn't using drugs, I would get into these fitness kicks—doing yoga and Pilates, and ultimately, weight lifting. It's funny to think about it now. One month I would be cooking and smoking meth and the next I would be all "namaste" on the yoga mat. Of course most addicts will tell you there is always a double life and a double lie.

Once I got clean and started the business, I again found my solace in fitness. I started really getting into weight lifting and in a lot of ways, it gave me the strength and inspiration to launch the business. If I could push 80 pounds above my head, I could also push the business to success. Weight lifting helped me to build that resiliency slowly over time as I was able to bench more, getting stronger day by day. It also taught me patience. Like with the business, it wasn't about overnight success. It was about practice; it was about hard work paying off.

Weights changed my relationship with my body as

much as that acid trip had—showing me a truth about myself I didn't realize before. Except this time, it wasn't amplifying a nightmare but a dream.

Once I realized I could change my body—that I had the power to make that kind of transformation—I believed I could do that anywhere in my life. In a perfect world, I would do yoga and Pilates and then lift weights; the combination slowed my body and mind down enough so I could sit with my thoughts and figure things out. That was important because, as I was about to learn, I had a lot more figuring out to do.

So there I was, eight years into the business with an eight-year old son. They were both my first babies in recovery. Things were going great financially—the bikini stands were killing it and Blissful Blends had established itself as a go-to stand in the Spokane community.

And yet, I felt like absolute shit.

I was 33. I was still battling my eating disorder. I was working out and being healthy, and as part of that healthy lifestyle, I started playing with a meat-centric diet. I was only a few months into it when I swelled up like a balloon.

I wondered why everything I ate made me fat. I scheduled an appointment with a doctor who wanted to put me on water pills and some other prescriptions but I didn't believe that was the answer.

Around the same time, I started getting calls from Connor's school.

Mike and I sat across from his teacher and she explained, "Connor's a sweet boy but we just can't seem to get him to pay attention."

It wasn't a new complaint. Ever since Connor was in preschool, he had struggled with attention issues. When all the other little kids were sitting in a circle, Connor would be unable or uninterested in participating in the task at hand. We had already put him in occupational therapy but the teacher was pushing for something more.

"I think it's time you consider medication."

It felt like a punch to the gut. Here I was almost 10 years off of methamphetamines and now I was being asked to put my eight-year old son on them. But I had been down this road before. Only six years earlier, my grandmother and I had been sitting in front of another teacher, discussing Jacob. We had put him on Ritalin as the teacher and doctors suggested and we felt like he was drugged the whole time. Jacob was now turning 13 and my grandmother had already caught him with pot. By 15, he would run away for the first time.

I decided it was time to try another approach—for both Connor and me.

I made an appointment for myself with a naturopath and she didn't offer me a prescription; instead she gave me a why. Why was I always swelling? Why couldn't I maintain a stable weight? Why was I always lethargic? Why did I feel like I was always getting sick?

And then she offered me the same "whys" for Connor. Why couldn't he sit still? Why couldn't he control his impulses? Why couldn't he pay attention? Why couldn't he complete simple tasks, despite how brilliant he was in so many areas?

I began to realize that gluten and dairy were my main culprits. The naturopath did a round of bloodwork and suggested I start by eliminating them. The only problem was, like a lot of people, I was on the Standard American Diet (SAD), which was based on bread and milk. Plus, I owned freaking coffee shops, where the baked goods came in fresh and free every morning.

But I was so tired of looking and feeling the way I did that I knew I had to try something. And I had another motivation. According to Connor's results, he was also gluten-intolerant. It became a lot easier when I realized I was doing it for both of us. I threw myself into our new diets, excited that I now had a way forward for me and my son that would allow us to heal ourselves from the inside out.

I changed everything that came into our house, refusing to buy foods that wouldn't support our dietary needs. Around the same time, I kept getting this pain in my arms and fingers. I went back to my primary care physician, who said it looked like early arthritis.

"Arthritis?" I asked.

"Well, it's presenting as arthritis. Likely you have what we call mixed connectivity disease. It's something we also usually see in older patients."

"But I'm only 33."

"It happens," he shrugged, reaching once again for his prescription pad. And once again, I threw that prescription in the trash.

I was able to remove gluten from our diets and started Connor on the supplements the doctor suggested. But I was still struggling with dairy.

I began to realize that once you start removing one toxin from your life, you become a lot more sensitive to the other ones. Every time I would have milk or cheese, it was like I could feel my arms and hands flare up. I decided that I could either be consumed by the doctor's diagnosis or take responsibility for it. I finally quit dairy and within weeks, the tenderness in my arms and hands began to dissipate.

And the eating disorder? Suddenly, it began to dissipate too. I wish I could say I know the magic formula but what I realized was that every time I felt too full, I had created this connection with fullness and purging. Once I removed the gluten and the dairy, I naturally began to shift my portions. I wasn't starving myself all day and then shoving a bunch of bread down. I had to be strategic about my food, eating smaller portions throughout the day.

Suddenly, I didn't feel full anymore and I didn't feel the need to purge.

Now, I know that the reasons for that healing go well beyond portion size. Over the previous 10 years, I'd also had to do the emotional work to prepare for that moment physically. I had started therapy and had been working to relieve the pain of my childhood, the guilt of my using and the trauma that still hung like a veil over most of my family. I had begun to release it so that I no longer needed to purge it.

Once I was able to also break the habit of overeating and feeling the need to get it out, Aunt Bulimia no longer served a purpose.

But the best part of our family's changes happened the next fall when Connor went to school. His food was controlled, his days were structured and he had a nearly perfect year. His new teacher, who has read his file, asked what happened.

"Did you place him on meds?" he asked, looking at his file to see if it had been noted.

"No," I smiled confidently. "We changed his diet."

Sadly, for so many people, that is the one thing they don't want to look at. And I understand. It took me years and a lot of pain to finally be willing to change it. And it's hard to get there if you haven't started the emotional work. I wish we could heal our bodies first but the truth is, our physical health is just a symptom of our mental health.

Until we can begin to heal our spirits, it's hard to find the strength and resiliency to heal our bodies. It's not easy to break our food habits. In fact, most of those habits have been with us since childhood. Numerous studies indicate that a significant percentage of people with eating disorders also experienced childhood sexual abuse.

Food is frequently the first escape. It offers a way out of ourselves before we have access to alcohol or drugs. After a long day at work or a shitty interaction with a friend or just an urge to indulge, hitting McDonald's for a giant serving of fries or saying "fuck it" and ordering pizza for dinner might be a lot less dangerous (and also a lot less illegal) than picking up drugs or alcohol, but I think the impulse comes from the same place. And whether we are abusing it or depriving ourselves of it, we learn that our relationship to food is all about control, and usually it ends with the food controlling us. I had lived years believing I was healthy but suddenly, I could see all the bad habits I accumulated over my life. My reliance on gluten and dairy as well as my binge and purge behaviors were all brought into the light.

What I discovered is that we all have histamine buckets in our body, and when we consume something we're allergic to, we drop more histamines in the bucket. The more allergies, the more histamines. Once that bucket overflows, we experience leaky gut, which affects everything from our intestines and bowels to our brain and nervous system. It's why I was both swollen and lethargic, why I would be constipated for days and anxious and depressed at the same time.

But again, that's why I am grateful for rock bottoms.

I am grateful to my body for swelling up, to my hands and arms for sounding the alarm. Because I couldn't continue to live in my own ignorance. And neither could Connor.

We could have taken the medication, just further masking the problems—but thankfully, that amazing naturopath showed us the "why" instead. I have no doubt that if we hadn't listened, we'd be in even worse shape today, probably taking a dozen prescriptions for illnesses and aches and pains that would keep popping up no matter how many times we went to the doctor.

A few months after I shifted my diet, I went back to my primary care physician. He was shocked by my transformation.

"What did you do?" he asked. It was really the same question that the teacher had asked.

I offered the same reply: "I changed my diet."

Quitting drugs was hard, starting a new business was brutal, letting go of my sons and learning to parent again was both heartbreaking and enlightening, but changing my diet was possibly the hardest thing I had ever done. And that's why it took me so long to do it.

I always say, do what you need to do based on where you're at right now.

Maybe you're ready to make the change. Maybe you're sick and tired of being sick and tired too. Maybe you've finally hit that physical bottom where you're waking up exhausted every morning, dying to go back to bed, dragging your body through the day, looking at yourself in the mirror and wanting more. Maybe you're giving your all to your husband, your kids, your extended family, your job—putting yourself last, again and again.

Or maybe it's just not time yet.

I had been too busy for too long to stop and look at myself. For years, I had been running myself ragged. I would burn out and then need to get myself up and running again. And every time, I could tell I was a little bit more diminished. I would try to ignore my body, hating what I was experiencing and yet unable to really make the changes I deserved.

And what I realized is that it was never about my body. It never is.

I see these young girls who hate what they look like and it just breaks my heart. We grow up being so hard on ourselves, thinking if we don't look "perfect," somehow we don't deserve to treat ourselves well. At this point, I could care less what I weigh. I know that weight isn't really evidence of good health. It is so nice to be grown up.

Because now, how I feel is what really counts and the craziest part is when I feel good, I look good. I have energy, more excitement in general—about my life, about work, about my children and my future.

Does that mean I'm perfect with my diet? Fuck no. Because life gets busy and sometimes I get behind on my shopping and then I don't have the right food at home or enough time to prepare it—and then I'm rushing through the day again, grabbing what I can. But just like with lifting weights, I know I have to be patient with myself. Healthy food habits take practice. They demand that you fall down sometimes and that you get back up. I could easily say, "Screw it, I messed up, why bother?" But I have begun to see the ebb and flow to my life. I know when I'm going through a particularly crazy period, I can say to myself, "It's okay, give yourself this week or even this month, and then get back on your diet." One of the amazing things about eating healthy is that while one "bad" meal isn't the end of the world, one plate full of lean protein and vegetables and other good stuff can set you off on a lifelong journey of treating your body the way it deserves to be treated.

And sure, I might feel like shit after one of those crazy weeks or months, but it's just a reminder that my diet works and that if I want to feel good, I need to return to it.

It isn't about making demands of ourselves. Yes, we

set goals and create a vision but we have to be kind to ourselves in the process. We have to learn to enjoy the process as much as the destination, a practice which injects more joy into everything we do.

As I began to shift my physical habits, I started doing the same with my work habits. I started doing vision boards and incorporating more of my spiritual practice in my work. For me, prayer has always been about having a conversation with someone who I believe has my back.

I would make deals with God, asking that He help me to get the next coffee stand or that He help Connor in school, and in return, I would give back. It sounds so silly but as long as I hold up my end of the deal, I find that it usually works.

In a way, it's like I'm negotiating a contract with God.

"God, if it's your will, this is what I am wishing and hoping for. If you can help me to achieve it, I will be sure to help those in need and share the abundance you bring."

If you don't make the deal, then how does God (or the universe, or the great energy of the world) know that you intend to offer something in return? On one hand, it helps me to articulate my desires, to be really clear on my intentions and plans, and on the other, it helps me to identify how I want to give back. Both sides of the agreement are about adding positivity to the world. I don't ask for anyone to be hurt or harmed. I don't ask for anything but more abundance and service in the world.

As I built my team at work and at home, I began to realize that there was a time to trust in yourself and a time to trust in other people. For too long, I had tried to do everything at the shops myself—filling orders, overseeing the sales, managing the staff and greeting the customers—and with each store I added, I tried to duplicate those efforts. But over the same period, I had also trained an amazing staff who could do all those things for me. I just needed to trust them more.

Early on in my coffee days, I had hired a girl to help me as a barista. I thought I could trust her but one day, I came in to find she had busted into the safe and stolen all the money. For years, I would remember that, thinking I was still a bad judge of character. But in addition to healing my emotional and physical health, I had also been healing my intuition. I had an incredible group of people around me and began delegating more of the work to them, giving me more time to focus on my family.

And, as I soon found out, my family needed me more than I realized.

7

FINDING THE RIGHT PERSON
CAN CHANGE EVERYTHING

Mike comes from a traditional family—he had a Christian upbringing and his parents are still married and what you would call "normal." Mike was the adventurous one in the family, leaving home and hitting the road while still in high school. He worked all over the country, visiting every state. But while I was using drugs on the streets, he was busy working, trying to build a future. We always say, if we had met each other years before we did, we would have hated one another. But we met at the perfect time.

When I think back on our first year together, I am still in shock. I was using drugs the whole time, but I was also making those small baby steps for change. I don't know how Mike saw past all the trauma and bad decisions, but I guess he also saw those baby steps. He saw me inching forward, trying to make better choices, trying to be a grownup, even when he had already been one for some time. I mean, don't get me wrong, Mike wasn't perfect either, but he was a bit further along on the path to maturity. I just had to catch up.

The thing about finding the right person is that it's not just about luck. It's about being open to new experiences. Like I said, I didn't want to go out with Mike at first. He wasn't my "style" and I didn't think I would find him attractive. It's funny now since my sister's nickname for him when we first met was the "hot construction guy." I could tell he was a stoner—hence giving me the wrong phone number—but other than that, I was convinced that he was just too normal for me.

And our first years together were hard. All I knew about relationships I had learned from Dave. I thought everyone cheated so I assumed that Mike would too.

Mike had never been in a major relationship before —he'd never been married or had kids. He hadn't even really lived with anyone. He was used to doing everything in his own way and on his own time. He would go out with friends and forget to call me, leading me to think he was out with someone else. I would be digging through his receipts or combing through his phone and he'd just be like, "What, babe?"

His nonchalance only made me crazier. I knew there was no way I could trust him because there was no way I could trust anyone. But I kept going, sticking to that promise I had made with myself early on: I would do the opposite of what I thought I was supposed to do.

So if I wanted to start a fight or make accusations, instead I would leave the room and go calm myself down. The truth was there was no evidence that Mike was doing anything behind my back. He was with me every night and I never saw him receive a suspicious text message, nor was there a call from a private number in the middle of the night.

When I would ask, Mike would just laugh and say, "Jeez, babe, it's hard enough handling you. You think I could manage someone else?"

I knew he was right. I was more than enough and Mike wasn't really the kind of the guy who could hide a second life. He was far too straightforward to pull something like that off. But like they say, if you spot it, you've got it.

I didn't trust Mike because I still wasn't ready to trust myself.

Like a lot of things, I was realizing that trust was also a practice. It wasn't something that I woke up with one morning, it was something that I had work on, that I had to grow like a muscle. And just like with fitness, there were times when I was really committed and there were times when I failed to show up.

We both struggled in the relationship during those early years, but having Connor guided both of us. We knew we wanted to do right by him and so we worked to make our relationship as healthy as possible to give him the home that I was unable to offer Joshua and Jacob. Over the years, as I grew the business, Mike stood by me even when he thought I was crazy.

I'll never forget his shock when I did my first $5,000 week at XXX.

"The freaking bikini stands!" he laughed.

"I told you they would be successful."

"It's not because of the bikinis," he told me. "It's because of you."

But over the next few years, our fairytale began to fade. We were both working too much. Our fights seemed to intensify while the attraction felt like it was fading. My old fears were aroused and I would become convinced that Mike was going to leave. I told myself that we were too different anyway, that it would be better if we were on our own.

By 2016, almost 10 years since we first got together and just a few months before Connor turned eight, I decided I'd had enough. We were now arguing all the time—sometimes it was about money or raising Connor. Sometimes it was about Jacob—who was now on the streets, using. Sometimes it was about the businesses.

I decided that if Mike wasn't going to move out, I would.

"Where are you going to go?" Mike asked, confused

as to why I felt the need to break up our family over what he felt were typical marriage disputes. Maybe had I not seen how such fights could escalate, I might have been able to minimize them too. But I knew the fighting wasn't good and it wasn't healthy.

I got a little apartment but spent many of my nights back at the house, trying to keep life as normal as possible.

I knew that Mike had watched his parents weather a number of storms; I had watched my parents unable to weather theirs. It was a wide chasm for us to cross together. Every time there was a fight, something inside me said, "Run." I didn't know how to manage the conflict. I was too terrified to stay present to the hard stuff.

But as I'd learned over the previous six months, life outside of our marriage could be even harder.

I looked over at him as he drove and said, "I don't want us to be a broken family. Look, Mike, I know I fucked up. I mean, I needed to move out. I know that. We weren't good. We weren't treating each other right. You and I don't know how to work through the problems; we just know how to fight."

He nodded his head in agreement.

"Can we try counseling?" I asked.

Mike didn't have any experience with counseling but he agreed, and though we weren't in marriage counseling for long, the fact that he was open to working through our problems helped me trust that we might actually be able get through them. He showed me that the existence of those problems didn't mean he was going to give up on me or our family. By the beginning of January, I had moved back home and things had settled into a new normal.

Moving out had given me the space to get better control of how the relationship was affecting me so that I wouldn't be so quick to react or lash out. Having that time also helped both of us get clarity on what we wanted and needed in the relationship. When we first got together, I was practically feral. But this time, I knew who I was and what I believed. I knew what I wanted our marriage to look like and I knew how I wanted to behave within it.

By the end of that year, I was back over the toilet bowl. In 2018, I had my fourth son—my second with Mike.

My mother had five girls and when I had Mason, Mike joked, "I guess we only need one more boy to catch up." I laughed at the time, but in 2020, we welcomed our son, Lincoln, my fifth boy.

Over the last two years, Mike and I have been stronger than ever. The stores have begun to run themselves—with the help of my amazing management team—and I'm able to be home a lot more and have a lot less stress. The stores are also all turning a profit now. For so many years, I was just increasing the risk without any real gains. The silent stress of that on Mike and me was nearly intolerable but once the stores started making money, that stress nearly disappeared.

It felt like we could laugh and dance again. Of course, things aren't perfect. I still feel the same fight-or-flight reaction when we get into an argument. Although we've gotten a lot better at resolving things, there is still a part of me that will always be hardwired for escape. But now I can work through that feeling instead of actually making a break for it.

Marriage is a lot like breastfeeding. You put in all this time and energy and emotional work and you don't get to see the results right away. You don't get to see the value of your efforts. Then slowly, like with children, you see your relationship begin to grow. Together, you begin to learn new things like communication, empathy and being able to say, "I fucked up and this is hard but I am going to stay here and make it work."

And sometimes when things get hard, I think back to Mike's olive branch: "I don't want us to have a broken family."

I know what that feels like. My blood family is still broken in so many ways. Mike and I have been building a family that is whole and healthy. And one of the things I've come to realize is that a broken family isn't necessarily one in which two people get divorced.

A family is broken when its members stop caring about each other, when they stop loving each other. When they grow so far apart that it feels like there's no way they'll ever be able to truly connect again. And whatever happens in the future, I know that the family Mike and I have built will never be broken. Whether we live happily ever after together or not, we'll always be a family.

8

CONFRONTING HARD TIMES
IF YOU LIVED THROUGH THAT, YOU CAN LIVE THROUGH THIS

AFTER MY LAST STINT IN PRISON, I KNEW MY LIFE WAS going to change—I knew it *had* to change. And while I had the will, I didn't necessarily have a way forward. During the years when other people are graduating from high school, going to college and taking the first steps toward becoming full-fledged adults, I was doing drugs, in a series of abusive relationships and not focused on much besides getting through the day.

It's not like I didn't learn anything during that time. I learned about what not to do and for a long time I let that be my guide: I would say no to things the old me said yes to, and I would say yes to things the old me wouldn't have even considered. By using my past to guide my future choices, I was setting myself up for success—not by pretending everything I'd been through was magically erased but by drawing upon the strength I had developed. "After all," I would sometimes say to myself. "I'm still here, aren't I?"

In a lot of ways, I wasn't successful despite my past —I was successful because of it. On the streets, you learn how to trust your instincts. If you get a bad feeling about a person, place or activity, it's probably because something bad is going to go down. The world of business isn't much different. Rather than let people intimidate me, I had to learn how to hone those instincts in a new setting. Where I come from, you're always studying people, trying to suss out their vibes— if they're going to steal from you or hurt you or fuck you over in some way. People in the sober world aren't so different! In treatment, too, I began to learn more about personality types and why people do the things they do. It's enabled me to end business relationships with people I felt were toxic and it's also brought me closer to people I know I can depend on—like my business partner, Stacy.

I knew that as much as I wanted to do everything myself, it wasn't going to work forever. And so I was throwing wet noodles at the wall, hoping something or someone would stick and I'd be able to share the workload of my growing business with someone else. And just like they say in fairy tales, I met Stacy and I just knew she was the One.

We went to lunch one day and I had this whole

speech prepared. I asked her, "What are you doing? What's your plan?"

"I don't know," she said. "I guess I'm just waiting for somebody to call me up and offer me a job." And she was laughing.

I said, "Well, here I am, honey, with your job and hopefully your whole entire future."

Ever since then, she's been on my team and I've been on hers—we work together and we want to see each other be the best versions of ourselves we can be. Stacy is the kind of person who has real integrity. She does good things when no one is looking because she's a good person. That's what I value in people—not that they're loyal to me for one reason or another but that they're genuinely trying to do the right thing even when it might be easier to do something other than the right thing.

And while I've met a lot of bad people who have done a lot of bad things, it's the time I spent learning to read people and to trust myself that led me to this partnership and this person who means so much to me.

But business isn't everything (though sometimes it feels like it might be, on days when I'm working for 12 straight hours while also coming up with ideas that I know are going to totally take over my life for the next few months). The fact is, I never really learned how to take care of myself. I mean, I knew how to get by, but treating myself right? My mind, my body, my spirit?

Confronting Hard Times | 101

That's not something you have a lot of time and energy for when you're running around doing drugs and shoplifting with your boyfriend. It's also not something you have time for when you're building a business, trying to break even every month so you can pay bills and invest in the next business and start the whole process over again.

Still, I learned something when I was sick and when Connor was diagnosed with ADHD. Taking care of yourself isn't a luxury. You have to do it or your body will literally fall apart. You won't be able to move forward or do anything without being, quite frankly, pretty miserable.

I don't get a lot of free time. In addition to the coffee shops, I'm trying to expand in a number of different areas—real estate and other investments. I'm starting a podcast where my business partner and I are going to get into how we do what we do. I'm shuttling my kids around to different activities and appointments, I'm checking in on all the businesses, I'm taking meetings. And while I've learned to loosen the reins a little bit and delegate some of my work to people I know and trust, the instinct to just do it all myself still exists and it's hard to tell myself no.

But I learned that I have to set those boundaries—not so much with other people (although that's important too) but with myself. So every day I have a routine: I get up, I work out, I shower. It sounds simple, but it's so easy to just get up and start working or start doing stuff for the kids or start doing anything other than something for yourself. By 11 in the morning, I'm ready to start the workday, and while I might technically be able to get more done if I used the hours between 8 and 11 am to work or run errands, I wouldn't function as well, which in the long run means I'd actually be less good at the things I care about.

Thinking back to the days when I was so sick and almost ready to say "fuck it" and start taking medication is a huge motivator for me. I know that's not a place I want to go back to, so I make the effort to not go there. I think so many people get through a hard time and think of it as behind them rather than something they can continue to learn from. And I don't mean to say that you have to dwell on the heavy shit all the time, because that's not the point! The point is that whatever traumas, heartaches, personal disasters and physical ailments you've experienced in your past are things you can and should tap into as sources of strength moving forward. Which, actually, is a great segue into my next point.

If you lived through that, you can live through this.

After everything I went through as a teenager and a young adult, it feels sort of crazy to say now that stress is the thing that almost killed me.

I mean, the list of things that could have killed me isn't a short one: between the drugs, my relationship with Dave and sleeping in some less-than-safe places, stress doesn't seem that bad. And on the surface, stress can almost feel validating—if I'm working so much that I'm stressed or my business is expanding so fast that it's causing me anxiety, isn't that ultimately a good thing? Doesn't that mean I'm succeeding?

Stress *did* almost kill me, though. Before I took a hard look at my body and my health, I was headed towards a place of being medicated and staying sick, and then getting so stressed about *that* that I'd make myself even more sick. And I'll say it again: making the changes I've made to my diet, my lifestyle and my mindset was the hardest set of changes I've ever had to make. At so many points, I didn't know if I was going to be able to do it. It seemed like it might be easier to give up.

But I didn't.

Saying "what doesn't kill you makes you stronger" is a cliché, but it's also true. I have lost and given up so much in my life: my mom, my boys. I've had to cut ties with people I loved and cared about because I knew if I didn't, they'd drag me down with them. I've put my body through hell.

And I'm still here.

I'm going to give myself a pat on the back here: that's pretty fucking incredible! Not just that I literally survived but that some part of me held onto hope that things could get better. Even when I didn't know it, somewhere in the back of my mind, my brain was holding onto that idea, waiting for the rest of me to be ready to hear it.

Part of why I'm even writing this book and sharing my story is that I want other people to see that I made it out alive. Because we all have things in our past, or even in our present, that we feel like we just can't escape or survive. It doesn't have to be a story as dramatic as mine either. Getting divorced, getting fired, losing a parent or a friend, even just feeling down or depressed for long enough: all of that stuff can so easily pull us down. But I think we have the power to change that narrative—to frame the things we've lived through as battles we've won. That's what I want for the women who work for me and the women who will listen to my podcast and the women who read this book: to see that you've survived, and that the jump from "surviving" to "thriving" isn't as scary as you think it might be.

Using the rock bottoms for growth and success.

I'm going to tell you a secret. There were times, even after the first coffee shops took off, that I wanted to quit. That I almost *did* quit.

I was, as you know, killing myself by working so hard and taking care of myself so poorly. The shops themselves were making a ton of money, but I was taking almost none of it. I was so focused on growing that when a coffee shop became profitable, I took those profits and put them right back into the next location. Increasingly, I was doing more jobs: in addition to hiring and firing and making schedules, I was also a bookkeeper, a real estate agent and an HR director. I was kidding myself if I thought this was a sustainable way to live, but since I had already lived so many *other* unsustainable lives, it was hard to give up.

And so I took a step back. I have a bookkeeper now and a business partner. Learning how to trust other people with my business was hard, and it's something I'm still working on. But I didn't have any other options.

I was talking with a friend recently, someone else in the coffee business, and she said "Sarah, I just don't know how you do it."

And you know what? It's fucking hard! But I'm doing what I have to do because I have no choice.

And so I told her, "You have to remind yourself that you don't have a choice. What else are you going to do? Who else are you going to work for?"

If you feel like there's a wall, then you have no choice but to do what you have to do to get over it. But every time I said to myself, "I can't manage people" or "We're not making enough money," or "Business is slow and I can't pay the rent" or even "Business is booming and I can't keep up," what were my options?

"If I can't figure this out, I'll have to quit."

And then I think about the times I've hit some kind

of rock bottom: when I gave up custody of my boys, when I went to prison (and when I went back to prison a second time). When I was so sick and so scared that I wasn't going to make it. And I think about how much I've been able to build on those foundations. Because that's the thing about hitting rock bottom: it's not a comfortable place to be. It's a rock, not a mattress or a trampoline. But it's *solid,* and it gave me the opportunity to really stand on my own two feet, no longer worried that the ground was going to swallow me up. I could look around and take stock of where I was and where I wanted to go, and then I could start to lay the foundation of my new life and my new home.

And everyone's rock bottom is different. You don't have to end up in prison to feel like you've truly hit bottom. In fact, I wouldn't recommend it! But there's some beauty in knowing that your rock bottom is *yours*. Because once you decide, once you know in your bones that you're there?

There's nowhere to go but up.

9

OTHER WOMEN AREN'T THE ENEMY
NO, NOT EVEN THE HOT ONES

I HAVE 10 COFFEE SHOPS NOW AND ONE OF THE THINGS I'm proudest of is how much customers genuinely love them. Think I'm exaggerating? Here, read some reviews people have left on Yelp:

Stopped here on the way when I moved to Seattle. Very friendly service, but more importantly had an iced white chocolate latte that was probably the best coffee I had ever consumed. I still have a lot of Seattle coffee ahead of me, but at times I contemplate driving all the way out there just for another coffee!

She was VERY nice and absolutely gorgeous! I ordered a triple 16 oz Mocha and asked for it to be just a little bit sweeter than usual. She made it PERFECTLY. It was Delicious!!

What a GREAT way to start the morning...Got a caramel latte, hot chocolate and some warm sandwiches. Service was fast and very friendly and the coffee was delicious!

Notice anything? How about the fact that all of these reviews make a point of saying how good the coffee was, how friendly the service was, how visiting one of our locations once made them for sure want to come back?

Do you also notice that none of these reviews say anything sleazy about the girls who work for me or about the shops in general?

In a way, I was both surprised and not surprised when the first wave of protests against Devil's Brew started to happen. On the one hand, I know how people are—they get nervous about anything even remotely associated with sex, sure that their children are going to go down an irreversible path of sin if they see girls working in one of my coffee shops wearing lingerie or fishnets.

But I also know myself, my business and the girls who actually wear the lingerie and make the coffee. I know that they're friendly and that our whole aim is to put smiles on faces and provide coffee just as good as what you'd get at any artisanal Seattle coffee shop—but with a little visual treat you definitely can't get anywhere else.

It's also not like I'm the first person in the history of

the world to think about using hot girls to sell food and drinks. In the 1960s, Playboy Clubs were after-work hotspots where high-powered businessmen could go—sometimes with wives and girlfriends! They'd drink martinis that were served by babes in the now-classic Playboy Bunny costume—cute and flirty with its iconic headband ears and white tail.

Then, in 1983, Hooters took the concept even more mainstream. Its restaurants, many of which are located in family-oriented areas, are known for serving up beer, wings, burgers and fries carried by upbeat, smiling girls in their signature uniform. You can probably picture it now: the white tank top with the owl logo, orange short-shorts, white socks and sneakers. The girls who work there are like grown-up cheerleaders, excited to have a good time at work and excited for you, the customer, to have a good time eating dinner. On any given Saturday night, Hooters might be filled with guys there to throw back beers, eyes popping out of their heads at the sight of hot girl after hot girl, but you're also just as likely to see grandparents, moms and dads—even whole families—stopping in to enjoy a lunch or dinner of all-American food served by all-American girls.

It's not like Hooters is the only game in town, either. There's a restaurant chain called Twin Peaks, where the girls wear flannel crop-tops and hiking boots, as well as a chain of bars called Tilted Kilt, where the uniform includes a sexy plaid miniskirt. If you talk to girls who work at these places, you'll find that nine times out of ten, they *love* their jobs. They make great money, sure, but they're also making customers happy, which, if you've ever worked retail or food service, you know isn't always the norm. Being a Hooters girl or a Kilt girl is like being in a sorority, and it's a huge honor to get chosen to represent the brands in calendars or at promotional events. To put on the orange shorts or the plaid microkilt is *cool*, and it's also a great way to put yourself through school or to save up enough money to move or help your family or whatever other goals you want to accomplish.

But enough about the history of this business. Let's get back to *my* business.

Remember when I said earlier that I knew I was going to be good at this?

On the first day I interviewed girls who wanted to work at what would become Devil's Brew, I thought I might've made a huge mistake.

I set up tons of interviews, and I knew I was going to have my pick of the litter. Smoking hot girls were going to be fighting over shifts—that's how I thought this was going to go.

At the end of that day, guess how many girls I'd met that I felt could represent me and my business the way I envisioned it?

Other Women Aren't The Enemy | 111

If you're laughing right now, so am I. The number, obviously, is zero.

I was crying hysterically. What the fuck had I gotten myself into? How had I ever been so confident? Where were all the cute, bright, coffee-making girls of my dreams?

Obviously, I didn't give up (this would be a totally different book if that were the case). It took time for me to build the team I wanted but it did happen.

By 2014, I was selling tons of coffee. And I seriously mean tons of coffee—my profits at the Devil's Brew location were easily double than they were at coffee shops where the baristas weren't dressed in their underwear and a smile. Some people, of course, weren't thrilled about my stores being so popular—or even about them existing in the first place.

A group of Spokane moms set out to collect 10,000 signatures to put the sexy coffee issue on the November ballot. The issue quickly blew up in the press, as local papers and news stations seized on the opportunity to feature an age-old story: young, sexy girls and the people who wanted them to cover up.

It was only a matter of time before the national news came calling. Some of the moms who were trying to shut me down (or at least get me to move out of my prime locations) talked to ABC reporters about why they were so fired up.

"My daughter just said, 'Mommy, look, there's a

lady without a shirt on,'" one woman told the channel, "and I was like, 'What?' So we all turned our heads and at that point, my three, five and seven-year-old were exposed to something that I would have never wanted them to see."

More than one person compared my coffee shops to strip clubs—which, by the way, they're definitely not. City council meetings were jammed with complaints. At one point, people were pushing for school busses to be re-routed so that kids wouldn't even catch a glimpse of…my store's sign. I don't actually know what these people thought kids would be able to see through a bus window and across the street, but I guess they didn't want to take any chances.

People were surprised to learn I didn't have a problem with this being brought to the city's attention. At the end of the day, I love that we live in a free country. It's everyone's right to be heard and the whole point of living in a democracy is that if you don't like something, you're free to try to change it.

But I would tell people who think my coffee stands and the girls who work in them are wrong or immoral or dirty the same thing I told ABC when they interviewed me for a segment on the controversy a few years ago:

This isn't about sex. It's about empowerment.

I'm not naïve. I know plenty of people come to my drive-thrus to see what the girls are wearing—or aren't wearing—on any given day. I know the girls who work for me are attractive, and I know for a lot of customers, that's way more important than the quality of my coffee (which, for the record, is pretty damn good).

But my girls aren't selling sex. I don't hire strippers and I actually have some fairly strict rules: no OnlyFans, no "extra" off-the-clock kind of work or super explicit social media. And it's not because I have anything against sex work—doing time in jail and in prison, I've met tons of women who were locked up for selling sex, and I still don't understand why it's illegal in the first place.

When it comes to my business, though, I'm looking for someone who wants something different. I always say my dream barista is a cute college girl, looking to work some shifts to pay for books, for classes, to invest in herself. Because it's also worth pointing out that I'm not the only one who makes more money through the sexy coffee stands than the more traditional ones. In addition to their hourly pay, a lot of girls who work for me report making something like $150 in tips per shift —for a 20-something girl working a part-time job, that's way better than she'd do at a fast-food joint or a big box store. And that kind of money, if you're smart about it, can quickly add up to freedom and opportunity: two of the things I value most.

I won't lie and say that every girl I've ever hired has been a model employee. In the early days, I was barely older than my staff—in some cases, by just a few years. Attractive girls plus lots of partying plus a mostly cash-based business is sometimes a recipe for disaster, and I've had situations where girls stole or quit and convinced all their friends to quit and work at another coffee stand, as well as times where I had to fire multiple girls at once. And it's hard because I do want to see the good in people, but I'm also street-smart enough to know what the signs of trouble are. I also won't say I was always the world's best boss: I'm tough on myself and I'm tough on employees. When I first started running the stands, I was also totally new to business, which meant I was totally new to managing people. But through working with business coaches and therapists, I've come to a place where I feel pretty good about my ability to lead. I also won't say that it's always been easy for me. I can be jealous when it comes to relationships —to the point where I've made myself sick imagining boyfriends even *looking* at other girls. Opening the first lingerie coffee stand was a real Come to Jesus moment for me. I thought, "Well, I'm either going to be successful or I'm going to let my insecurities hold me back." And instantly I felt a lot of my old insecurities melt away: they had been so strong for so long, but it was like my brain and my body knew they were going to get in the way of my success, and so they had to go.

Most of the girls who work for me take pride in

their jobs. Our customers aren't just men—they're families, moms with kids, women heading to work in the morning. Everyone is served just the same, receiving a huge smile from the barista as they pick up their coffee. We also work to keep the menus fresh—right now we've got pumpkin spice lattes, chai tea, even flavors like lavender. Because I don't want to rest on the fact that my baristas are good-looking and wearing skimpy outfits—I genuinely want people to like what we're selling and to keep coming back.

In a sense, that's what I want for my employees too. I've done enough time and seen enough things to know the signs of trouble: when someone might be partying too much, working too little and generally not honoring her commitments to others and to herself. But because I've been there, and because I've pulled myself out of that place, I also know about the other signs too: the single mom determined to give her kid a better life than the one she had, the girl going to school at night and working two jobs so that she can become a teacher, a doctor or a lawyer. And the girls who work for me know about my story too. They know I'm there for them to offer advice or support and to show them that it can be done. A lot of girls who work for me describe us as a family and I'm proud of that. I'm proud of the fact that I work with them to make sure they're getting to class on time or they're able to take time off to be with their sick kids without worrying about getting fired.

My baristas definitely aren't there to steal anyone's husband or boyfriend, and that's clear to anyone who buys coffee from us regularly. They actually have fun at work—we have theme days with special outfits. They get to know the likes and dislikes of customers—who hates whipped cream, who works the night shift and who needs a cookie or a muffin on their morning drive.

In a lot of ways, I'm lucky to be alive let alone thriving as a woman, a mom and a business owner. And while I made a lot of that luck myself, I was also fortunate enough to have help along the way in the form of people who believed in me, people who gave me a chance to prove that I was more than my history and my record. I took my life and my future into my own hands and that's what I want for my employees. They're making an honest living—how can that be anything other than empowering and inspiring? At the end of the day, I can teach anyone how to make a great latte or pick an outfit that strikes the exact right balance of sweet and sexy.

But being thirsty for change, the same way I was? That's something the girls bring on their own, and I, for one, think that's something to celebrate.

10

LOOKING FORWARD
FOCUSING ON MY FAMILY AND MYSELF

When I was younger, I didn't spend a lot of time thinking about the future. I mean, how could I? When you're doing drugs, so much of life revolves around getting the next fix. When my friends and I were out running the streets, we had to figure out things like where we were going to sleep that night and what we were going to eat.

And even when I started running my first coffee stand, it was hard to think beyond just getting through each day. With so much to learn, I didn't have time to think about the Sarah of 10 years from now. I barely had time to think about the Sarah of that day!

But when I think back, even as far back as when I was a little girl, there is one vision that I always kept with me.

I wanted a family.

It didn't matter how many kids there were, if they were boys or girls, or even what they looked like. I just knew they would be my family, and I held tight to that image even in my darkest moments.

And now, all these years later, I'm really doing it. In addition to Connor I have a two-and-a-half year-old and a nine-month-old, and being their mom is one of the most important things I've ever done.

It's also *really fucking hard*.

I mean:

Every day, I get up, get them fed and get Connor to school. Soon the younger ones will be in school too and that will be three sets of teachers to manage, three sets of classrooms to keep up with. Lunches, birthday parties, colds, bumps and bruises. And that's the easy part! Because I want to give my kids what I didn't always have. I was lucky that even when things were really bad at home, I knew there were people who loved me. But I want so much more for my kids. I want them to be safe, I want them to be secure and I want them to be free. To make mistakes and know that those mistakes won't define them. To make mistakes and know that I'll still be there. And while I know that everyone learns some lessons the hard way, I don't want them to learn in the hard ways I learned.

So what does this actually look like?

I don't call myself a feminist. When it comes to relationships, I'm honestly pretty traditional, hard as that may be to believe. But I think women are total badasses. There's so much shit women go through that men can't even imagine! And so part of raising a family for me, especially as my business expands, is surrounding myself with other women who are just as focused and determined as I am. One of the things I love about my business partner Stacy is that she's a working mom too and we're able to talk about all of these things with each other.

At the coffee shops, of course, almost all of my employees are women and it's important to me to offer them support as they raise their own kids. When one of my baristas is having a baby, I want her to take time off to rest and bond with her infant and not worry about losing her job. I want to be a business that supports women and that lets them live their lives because so much of who I am is tied closely to my family and my kids. If my kid has the day off from school, he might come to work with me, and I feel proud that I was able to build a life for myself where that's something I can do.

I also have childcare help, which I'm not shy about saying! I know having help, whether it be paid or in the form of friends or grandparents or even a stay-at-home spouse, isn't an option for everyone. I know how lucky

I am that my work allows me the flexibility and the income to have someone take care of my kids when I'm racing around town, coming up with new business ideas and then hustling to make them a reality.

I also know that even though I can afford to hire help, there are a lot of people who would say that I shouldn't. That a mom's role is to stay home and take care of the kids, and that to want to work outside the house, to have an identity other than "mom," is selfish. But you know what? Fuck that! Running my businesses makes me a better mom in so many ways. Rather than feel guilty about having a nanny,—who, by the way, is incredible at her job—I want to focus on the things it makes possible for me and my family.

First, it means I know my kids are well taken care of. Nothing is more important, more precious to me than them, and in my nanny Katie I know I have someone who cares for them and puts their well-being first.

Second, it means that I'm able to have them be accessible to me throughout the day. When I'm working from home, which I often am these days, they're there. This is a blessing and a curse, of course. I love getting to see them and soak in this time with them, but it also sometimes makes even sending texts and emails take twice as long.

Having someone I trust with my kids also means something that I think is really important: when I'm at work, I'm at work. I'm able to totally focus on the business I'm doing. Whether it's hiring a new employee, looking at a new piece of real estate or meeting with a potential new partner, I'm 1,000 percent there. And that, in turn, makes me a better mom. Money is part of it—I'm investing in this work so I can take care of my kids and set all of us up for success.

But I'm also showing my kids what hard work looks like. What it looks like to be accountable and responsible—the good, the bad and the ugly. To rely on yourself rather than waiting for someone to take care of you. That's one of the greatest gifts I can give them, and it's why I'm so passionate about helping the women who work for and with me have as much of a work-life balance as they can. And look, I know that's going to be different for everyone and every family. Hell, it even looks different in my own family depending on what day of the week it is.

My kids have grown up—and, in the case of the younger ones, are still growing up— differently than I have. They've also grown up differently from each other. And—if you're sensing that this is a theme, you're probably right—my relationships with all of them aren't perfect. But I love those relationships more than words can express. Each of them, in their own ways, saved my life. I'm impulsive and I have a tendency to dive into things headfirst. With my kids, though, I'm not just thinking about myself. Because they need me, and I'm going to be there for them no matter what.

Part of being the best mom I can be also means that for the first time in my life, I had to learn how to take care of Sarah. That started, crazily enough, the second time I went to prison.

Prison was a turning point for me. The second time I went in, I had some sobriety under my belt and I'd started, in some small ways, to think about what I truly wanted out of my life. I knew that what I did *not* want out of life was to spend more time behind bars, cut off from the world, so I tried to make the most of my time inside. I worked the programs, the meetings and the counseling. Like I said earlier, I also spent a lot of time in the library, hungry for any kind of knowledge that might help me climb out from where I was.

Here's a question, though: did I deserve to be there in the first place?

According to the law, I very much did deserve to be locked up. But why is the law the way it is? While I was there, I met a girl who was arrested after she got drunk, crashed her car and killed her best friend, who had been sitting in the passenger seat. Can you imagine carrying the weight of that on your shoulders for the rest of your life? What would being in prison do for this girl? Wouldn't that just punish and not rehabilitate her?

I've come to believe we need massive prison reform

in this country. The system, as it is, is broken, offering little to no chance for people who get caught in it to actually develop the tools they need to live life on the outside. Prisons themselves could be doing so much more. The one I was sent to was the size of a college campus. It was big enough to have had a huge garden and space for more classes or job trainings.

Tons of people make tons of money off of prisons and prisoners in this country, which incentivizes a setup for people to get caught in the cycle of recidivism rather than rehabilitate out.

And it should go without saying that I'm not talking about violent criminals here, people who seriously hurt and abuse other people. I'm talking about girls who do drugs, kids who shoplift. Is the system helping them get better or is it making them worse? I had to go to prison twice to decide I wanted something different for my life and I still have nightmares about it, my sleeping brain coming up with visions of getting sent back for five or 10 years.

So: the system needs fixing because it doesn't work. I believe that. I did things and made choices that landed me in prison, not once but twice.

And for me to have made the progress I've made, to have come this far?

I had to own it.

One of the single most important forces in my life is personal responsibility. And it's not about beating yourself up and feeling guilty for bad things you've done or hurtful things you've said to people. It's about being honest with yourself. Because only when you're really telling yourself the truth can you start to take control.

When you start to think about personal responsibility in those terms, as a way of taking control of your own life, it pops up everywhere. All those books I read in prison? The words might have been different, but they were all telling me the same thing, and I haven't forgotten it now that I'm out. Here's how it breaks down for me.

I matter.

Try saying those words to yourself.

Do you believe them? When you look in the mirror, do you see a person that matters? Not to other people, but to yourself?

For a long time I wasn't sure if I mattered. I might have treated other people badly, but there's no one I treated as badly as myself. I was treating my body, my heart and my mind carelessly and it showed. At every moment something went right for me, it's been a moment where I believed that I, Sarah, mattered. When I had my abortion and that small voice planted the seeds of change in my head? That was me accepting that I mattered. When I just *knew* I would be good at running the first coffee stand, and every coffee stand after that? I mattered. And when I saw the positive pregnancy test so early on in my relationship with Mike and I knew that I was going to have this baby and be the best mom I could be? *I mattered.* It was only through taking responsibility for myself—the best parts of me and the worst parts of me—that I could begin to see myself in this new way. So often, we as women put ourselves last by default. Our needs can only be met after everyone else's needs are satisfied. Personal responsibility is a gift that allows us to tell all that noise to shut up. To take charge of our own needs, our wants, our *lives*.

Part of taking charge is owning the not-so-great things I may have done in the past, but there's real joy in it too. Because when I'm taking charge and accepting responsibility, I'm also saying to the world and to myself that I have the power to build the future I want for myself and for my kids.

Katie, my nanny, sometimes laughs when I talk about the people I keep up with on YouTube.

"It's like they're your friends," she says, and she's not wrong—I love to see who has a cute new boyfriend, who got a dog, whose kids made the football team.

And I watch a lot of people who are interested in the same stuff I'm interested in—writing your own story, literally speaking your goals into existence.

Which is why I recently found myself cracking up while watching a video about scripting, which is the idea that you can have anything you want if you're willing and ready to say, out loud, that you want it.

"Holy shit," I said to myself.

"I'm going to make 10 million dollars this year!"

And I believe that I can! Every year, I make a vision board. It sounds cheesy, but it helps me get my thoughts organized and set goals I want to achieve. But when I was making this year's vision board, I had this feeling that came out of nowhere which said I wasn't thinking big enough. So now my vision board says I'm going to make 10 million dollars this year and it's going to say that every year until I decide I'm ready to reach bigger.

It's not only about the money—though of course I can't wait to be making 10 million dollars a year. It's about speaking up and saying out loud what I'm going to do. And when I look back, haven't I been doing that for the last decade? I said I was going to stop doing drugs, I said I was going to quit throwing up my food, I said I was going to make my business a success. If I didn't have the courage, the guts, to say those things out loud, I don't think they would have come true. Because when you stay quiet, nothing changes. You don't change. Speaking up is making a promise to yourself, that whatever it is you want—from the smallest goal to huge, life-changing opportunities—you're going to get. You will!

I have this vision in my head of a little old lady in

huge, Coke-bottle glasses. Her hair is done, she's rocking the hottest fashions for 80-year-olds and you can tell from looking at her that she's lived an awesome life.

I want that to be me. I know that's going to be me, actually, because I'm here telling this story. It's so easy in life to stay quiet. To go with the flow, to do what other people expect of you and give them what they want from you. But when you hit rock bottom, there's one good thing you lose, and that's the part of you that cares too much about what other people think. And when that happens, you can start to speak up! What do you think? What do you need? What do you want?

Women, especially, are socialized to keep quiet, to not use our voices. And even now, it's not always easy for me. I have a business partner that I was pretty hard on and I'll never really forgive myself for how rude I was to him. But he tells me all the time, "Thank you for that, you taught me so much. You taught me you've got to be an asshole sometimes to get what you need."

And it's not like I want to be an asshole all the time. There have been days where I've thought about quitting because I saw myself becoming a person I didn't want to be. A person who was short with her staff and her family, a person who was angry all the time.

"I want to be successful," I would think, "but at what cost?"

I want to have good, healthy, loving relationships. I

want to be happy! I *don't* want to be "that bitch with the coffee" or worse. But I also don't want to be someone who doesn't use her voice, because there's so much power in using your voice.

Think about the voice that told me, all those years ago, that maybe there was something else out there for me. The voice that told me to buy the first coffee stand. The voice that told me to expand the business. The voice that told me to take a look at what my son and I were putting into our bodies. These voices weren't coming from nowhere—they were coming from *me*. That was *my* voice, pushing me to grow and change not so that I could be some hot, rich lady with a business empire (though I obviously wouldn't say no to that), but so that I could become a person who shows other people how awesome life can get when you learn to listen, and you learn to speak.

I've wasted so much time worrying about what would happen if I asserted myself. But what actually happens when you assert yourself? People listen, because you're not giving them a choice! This doesn't mean that you're going to start telling people things and having them immediately do what you want them to do all the time. That's definitely not how it works in my life. But when you assert yourself, people respect you. More importantly, you respect yourself. You become a person who takes control of her own life, and who gets shit done for herself and the people she cares about.

Now that we're nearing the end of this story—which in a lot of ways is also just the beginning—you might be wondering how I took everything I've been through and turned it into a story. Into my story, the one from which I draw strength and the one with which I sincerely hope to inspire anyone who thinks they don't have what it takes to break free of whatever prison they're stuck in. It's been a long road. Because one thing I don't have these days is a ton of time to be by myself and just think. Or even to *not* think, to just zone out and see where my mind goes.

I do work out, though, and that usually gives me that freedom. I put my music on—hair metal from the '80s, classic hip hop, Eminem, whatever I'm feeling that day. And I just let my mind do its thing.

That's a huge gift I've given myself, and in a lot of ways it's how I ended up here, writing this book. For so many years, I was focused on putting one foot in front of the other every day. Was I going to make it through whatever shitty situation I was stuck in? Was I going to serve my time in prison without going totally insane? Was I going to make enough money at my first coffee stand to stay afloat? Was my body going to stop hurting so much?

Not a lot of time for introspection there.

I've actually been talking with one of my sisters

recently about starting a family podcast. One that dives into all the things that happened during our childhood, how we each reacted to them and how they affect us now. And whether it actually happens or not, it's incredible to me that I've come to a point in my life where I can really go there, with myself and for other people.

Because that's a huge part of all of this. I want to be the best version of myself for my kids, for my employees, even for myself—to show myself every day that I'm doing the best I can. But I also believe that when I woke up and felt those first pangs of thirst for something different, that a huge part of that was for a purpose beyond myself.

I read these books written by professional thinkers and therapists and life coaches that say: "This is how you do it." Everyone has different stories and tells their stories in a different way, but it's always a little bit like watching a movie you could swear you've seen before.

We're all doing the same thing. Whether your lows are as intense as my lows, we're all hitting various bottoms and trying to figure out how to climb back out. And seriously: if you're able to read a book and learn from someone else's experiences without having to go through it all yourself, do that. I did it the hard way but that doesn't mean that you have to. Once that thirst takes over, the change you're looking for is going to come, one way or another. Because you're going to make it happen.

But if I have any closing advice? Take a shortcut! Read a book!

And look at that—you just finished reading this one. You're already on your way.

ACKNOWLEDGMENTS

Dad - Thank you for the many times you put your success on the line for mine. You believed in my abilities long before there was evidence of change. You've always encouraged my next steps forward. You gave me the gift of sarcasm and the ability to laugh through the tough times, all while crying with me.

Mom - Thank you for knowing me better than I knew myself. For creating such a defiant and fighting spirit in me. Your heart was so big it could never be filled. The lessons you taught me were huge. I love you and I miss you.

Josh & Jake - Thank you for the unconditional love and forgiveness. Without it, I don't know if I could have forgiven myself and become the mom I am today. I am forever grateful. I am here to love and support you through the good and bad, forever and ever.

Grandma - You are the rock of the family; you never let us fall apart even when it seemed impossible to keep it all going. You taught me perseverance and I can't imagine where this family would be without you! You are my idol and I hope to be just like you when I grow up.

Connor - You are the first kiddo I got to take home and you've never left my side. You give me purpose and continue to make me proud! I have learned so much with you and I still can't believe how intelligent and funny you are. I can't wait to see what you go on to accomplish. I believe in you.

Mike - Thank you for always demanding I do better and questioning what I know. You made me a fucking encyclopedia and I come well prepared because if it. You keep me digging for more knowledge to this very day. You always support me and my wild ideas and I love you always. You gave me three beautiful babies and even though we didn't raise Josh & Jake, you continue to be there for them even when it's tough.

See - You have one of the biggest hearts I have ever seen. You believe in people. You fight for people. You show unconditional love. You have been my mentor and have paved the way for me, allowed me to be a part of the family and given me the tools to truly better my life. Your kindness made me want to live up to the potential you saw in me. I hope to make you proud. You taught me the importance of giving back. I am so grateful to have you in my life.

Freddie - Thank you for believing in me when no one else did. And for forcing me to write my first business plan! I learned so much from our first business deal. I don't think I ever told you how many people I asked to invest in me before I ran into you. I can't count. You really set this whole thing off and I am forever grateful. Many more to come.

Anna & Launch Pad Publishing- Without at doubt, this wouldn't have happened without you! You've held my hand every step of the way in this long and emotional process. You took care of every detail and really made this entire process seamless. You gave me a voice and I couldn't thank you more. I can't wait to start on number two. C'mon girl, you know I can't stop at one!

Finally I thank everyone in my story, good or bad. You held my feet to the fire and formed the person I am today. I am grateful I met every single one of you. I forgive you and I hope you can find it in your heart to forgive me.

ABOUT THE AUTHOR

Born and raised in Washington, Sarah Birnel is the owner of two chains of stands—six under the Bliss Coffee umbrella and six under the Black Sheep umbrella—as well as the salad restaurant Always Fresh & Foraged. A former prisoner, she transformed her life at 22, eventually turning a job at a local coffee stand into an empire based on the leadership, sexiness, strength and drive of women. Her goal with all her female-employed businesses is to provide a space that accommodates the demands women have personally, at home and at work so they can "have it all." Birnel lives in Spokane with her children.